What Customers Really Want

Published by :
Lotus Press Publishers & Distributors

What Customers Really Want

Keshu Patnaik

4735/22, Prakash Deep Building
Ansari Road, Darya Ganj,
New Delhi - 110002

Lotus Press Publishers & Distributors
Unit No. 220, 2nd Floor, 4735/22, Prakash Deep Building,
Ansari Road, Darya Ganj, New Delhi-110002
Ph.: 41325510, 98118-38000
• E-mail : lotuspress1984@gmail.com
www.lotuspress.co.in

What Customers Really Want

ISBN: 81-8382-169-3

Printed & Published by : **Lotus Press Publishers & Distributors,** New Delhi-02

PREFACE

'What do customers really want?'—This is a question which has plagued many a diligent businessman, since the very beginning of trade and commerce itself. While most entrepreneurs prefer to adher to age-old practices of giving customers and clients what they always have had, contemporary market trends dictate otherwide. The marketplace today is not just a local place; it is the whole world. As such, with breakneck, stiff competition being the order of the day, conventional business products and services, unless gazed with unique marketing skills or enticing offers, hardly stand a chance of working in the long run mere. Commercialisation today has run its course and today's customer is a pampered trade patron with a befuddling variety of choices. In such a scenario, a smart entrepreneur must acknowledge the need for providing customers something unique, which crosses the boundaries of convention, and leaves both parties happy.

This book, recognising the need for such a manual handbook caters to the need of businessmen and women for a which gives them an insight into the mind of clients and customers. Constant improvement and change is inevitable to business growth, and a truly smart entrepreneur not only aknowledges it, but employs it and taps its potential to the fullest.

Providing insight into contemporary market ethics, trends and challenges, the book confronts questions of customer service values, and how relevant they are to the modern, savvy businessperson. Considering the incisive informtion and insight of the book, it is hoped that the book serves resourceful for the readers.

Editor

CONTENTS

1

IMPORTANCE OF CUSTOMER SERVICE

Customer service is the interaction you and your staff have with your customers. However, to fully understand this point, you must identify your customers. An error frequently made in this process is thinking that customers are only those clients who purchase your products or services. This is an incorrect view that will impact your business negatively. Sure, clients who pay for products and services are customers but they are not the only ones.

Customers that require customer service include just about everyone you encounter from fellow team members to sales prospects. If one of your assignments is to provide another staff member with a report, then that staff member is your customer and deserves the same level of customer service that someone purchasing a product or service would receive.

Customer service should not simply meet the minimal needs of a client or customer. The goal should be to delight that customer so that they will remember the contact as exceptionally pleasant and look forward to the next opportunity to interact with your business. When considering customer service, remember that any person who has a great experience with your business will potentially tell one or two people about the experience, giving you great word of mouth advertising. However, any person that has a negative experience with your company will also certainly tell a dozen people. People tend to share the negative more often than the positive experiences in their lives. While it may seem unfair, it is still a fact of doing business. This makes it very important to provide customer service, even when dealing with difficult people, that makes the people remember you in a positive light and share only good information about your operation.

EXCEPTIONAL CUSTOMER SERVICE

Today's marketplace is so competitive that without meeting and exceeding the expectations of client's many will never return for repeat business. To provide exceptional customer service is every company's goal. But all too often the staff and even the management of the business have no idea how to achieve this goal. Today's marketplace is so competitive that without meeting and exceeding the expectations of client's many will never return for repeat business. And it is repeat business that can allow a company to thrive.

To provide exceptional customer service, you must first earn the trust of your client base. If your clients trust you and have a sound business relationship with you, they will enjoy doing business with you. It doesn't matter if the contact is by telephone, email, face to face or through advertising, it must be an experience that builds trust through factual information that is provided in a friendly, caring manner.

To build trust in your customer service, always provide communication with straight talk rather than slick sales talk. Make your claims clear and honest and then provide exactly what you say you will provide. You'll also have to adopt a customer service posture that lets the client know that you are on their side. Don't be pushy and make sales through pressure. This will only lose trust for your company. Sometimes, it is better to tell a client that you can't provide them the best possible deal than to tell them a half-truth or badmouth another business, which will cause a breach of trust.

Building trust means providing customer service that protects your client's privacy and personal information. Today, with identify theft being such a problem, you must be able to ensure clients and buyers that you will never allow their information to get into the wrong hands. Then follow through by implementing policies and procedures that will ensure that privacy is maintained.

Another way to provide exceptional customer service is to create scenarios that will ensure your clients are passionate about your service. This means you have to provide the products and services that are needed by your customer base and provided in a way that can't be matched by other companies. Customer service should involve letting your clients know why your product is a better, less expensive and superior product than others. Give clients new ideas about how to use products and services and provide a menu of these that will meet the needs of a broad base of clientele. Make your service so great that customers will become passionate and loyal users of your products and services.

In every customer service situation, you must exceed the expectations of clients. Delight each and every client and those customers will return for more products and services. Never settle for doing the minimum. Go above and beyond in every situation. Be proactive; fix anything that isn't right even before the customer brings it to your attention. Then notify them that the problem has been corrected. They'll be delighted that they didn't have to call the problem to your attention.

Providing minimal customer service will result in minimal loyal customers. Providing exceptional customer service will build your business organisation and allow it to grow to new heights.

USING SATISFACTION SURVEYS

Customer service satisfaction surveys are a great way to learn how effective your company's customer service organisation and representatives really are from the viewpoint of the client. It doesn't matter what type of business you operate, whether it is a service company or a provider of products, you can implement this simple, cost-effective technique to measure the success of your service to customers and clients.

In order for customer service satisfaction surveys to be successful, they must be short and to the point. Five questions is a good length, but don't make the survey more than ten questions at the most. If it takes more than a minute or two to fill out the survey, many people will simply neglect to take the time, losing valuable input for your business organisation.

Make the questions on your customer service satisfaction survey clear and allow the customer to provide feedback on a scale of one to five with one being completely dissatisfied and five meaning delighted with the outcome.

Questions to include on the survey include asking the customer if their problem was resolved to their satisfaction. Also, ask them if this is their first contact to resolve this issue. These are important measurements to learn if your customer service is fast and effective. If a client has found it necessary to repeatedly contact your business to resolve a problem, then work needs to be done. If they did not get the problem resolved, then research into the matter needs to be done to learn it this can be corrected.

Another point to bring out on a customer service satisfaction survey is to learn if the client found the quality of the product or service to be at fault. It is also important to learn the name of the representative that served this customer, both in the initial contact and in the customer service situation. Provide a space on the customer service satisfaction survey that the client can write in comments. These will allow you to learn much more about the situation and whether the service provided was flawed. Collect these surveys and gather the information. Identify strong points in your customer service and identify the areas that need improvement. Then, using the results from your customer service satisfaction survey, develop training and skills assessment to help your organisation improve the level of service provided to customers and clients.

CREATING GOOD RELATIONSHIPS

Online or off, good customer service is essential if you hope to maintain good business relationships. In order to maintain good relationships, you must be able to look at the customer as your cash cow and you also need to look at them as an acquaintance you look forward to seeing each and every time you see them.

Good customer service is essential for those of you in business for yourself. If you aren't providing your customers with good service, then usually your competitors will gladly take care of the job for you. Good customer service training is essential for all of your employees. Top companies throughout the world offer some of the best training programmes which can be very costly but they do it because they realise in order to have customers, they must take care of them so they are willing to put extra money into customer service training employees in the area of pleasing customers or providing customer satisfaction to the best of their abilities.

The employees of some reputed companies are put through extensive training and taught to handle the customer to the best of their ability. If they aren't able to handle customers to the customer's satisfaction, then representatives know they risk the customer taking their business somewhere else and in that case, their jobs aren't safe. If more companies drove that point home, then more companies would be more customer-driven just like them and their competitors.

Customer service representatives throughout the world know that they can offer good service to customers or bad service and they recognise the consequences of each. Employees of companies which provide good customer satisfaction are rewarded for their efforts and the people who don't offer good customer service, are not. It's really that simple. Companies are looking for employees who are company employees and company-driven as much as customer-driven. Taking care of the company's customers is essential for every customer service representative.

AVOID NEGATIVITY IN CUSTOMER SERVICE

To provide great service, avoid negativity in customer service. What exactly does this mean? It simply means to avoid focusing on negative outcomes and negative communications. In order to make this important process operate effective, customer representatives must be empowered to act on problems but it will create customer loyalty and repeat business for your organisation.

When a client contacts your business, either by telephone or in person, the last thing they want to hear is, 'I can't do anything about this matter,' or, 'no, that is against company policy'. Of course, at times company policy has to come first but it is simply a matter of communicating in a non-negative way.

When the client initiates contact, the first statement that he or she should hear from a representative of the business is, "I can and will help you". From that point only, the resolution of the problem should be given priority and done in a positive, caring manner. No matter how frustrated the client may be with the situation, the problem will be diffused if everything that is communicated to them involves positive statements, positive actions and positive attention to their needs.

Words that need to be avoided to avoid negativity in customer service include: no, never, not, impossible, unlikely, not normally, unable, incapable, can't, won't, shouldn't, not until, not at this time, not in my power, not permitted, out of scope, and anything else that sounds negative. Worlds like can, will, shall, immediate, right now, able to, within my responsibilities, normally, empowered, and other positive words must be used to communicate that something will be accomplished by the contact.

Of course, there are times that the desired outcome is not within the empowerment of the employee, but even that can be communicated in a positive manner. "I will immediately contact the person that will determine the cause of the breakdown and will immediately rectify the situation," is a positive way of saying that a person simply doesn't have the power to do what is needed. This statement leaves the customer with a good feeling, unlike a negative statement such as, "I am not authorised to do anything about this so I'll try to see if anyone can make the time to fix this problem and maybe they'll let you know."

Of course, positive customer service statements won't work unless there is follow-through and the situation is truly rectified. You can avoid negativity in customer service but unless the problem is resolved, the customer won't care how many positive words were used. The point, however, is to let the client know that the company cares and will do what is needed to make it right for the client if the company has failed to perform or provided a less than quality product.

If you train your staff to avoid negativity in customer service and train them to treat every person both inside and outside the organisation with respect and good manner, you'll be amazed at how painless many difficult situations can become. Speaking in a positive manner doesn't cost a thing except a little empathy and caring and it does bring profits in terms of customers that respect your products and services and come back again and again.

TIPS TO EFFECTIVE CUSTOMER SERVICE

Customer service jobs are stressful and many times you will find that the jobs within the area of customer service just leave a lot to be desired. The days are long and the hours often creep by when its just be one of those days. Here are some tips to help you remain focused and calm while dealing with people in customer service:

— Remember, it's just a job. No matter what happens during the course of the day, you still get to go home at the end of the day to relax with your family. This is only temporary and it is just a job. Dealing with customers and their complaints is just a small little increment in your life. So what if they told you off. You didn't know the person before they walked up and you have no desire to know them now. They are basically nothing in your life. So smile and thank them for shopping at V-Mart or wherever it is that you work.

— Never let a bad day at the office ruin your day at home. When you leave work, leave it at the door. If you want to pick it back up on the next day in, then fine but don't take a bad day home with you because it is your only safe haven.

— Customers are always right even when they are wrong and there is a way to master making them feel like they are right yet letting them know you know they weren't but you can do it without making anyone mad. So smile and thank them for making the world a better place.

— Focus on what the customer wants when they are in front of you. Hang on their every word and try to get them satisfied so you can move on to the next one as quickly as possible. If you are quick to handle customers with friendliness yet rapidness you don't set yourself up to have to listen to things you likely don't want to hear about.

— Take your breaks. When you deal with the public, you need to be able to walk away for a moment and regroup. Do this when it is scheduled because everyone needs and deserves a break. Also, if you start skipping your breaks then it becomes expected and you'll be sorry you started it at all!

— Know when to give up. You will never please everyone all of the time. Even the best customer service representatives realise this so shake it off and go on if you can't. If they won't go away, pass them off then smile, and know you won't be the one dealing with the customer for a while.

Being a customer service representative is tough. However, if you will learn to smile and laugh things off, you'll enjoy your career a lot more than if you vent too much over the little things in life.

2

RULES FOR GOOD CUSTOMER SERVICE

Improving customer service involves making a commitment to learning what our customers' needs and wants are, and developing action plans that implement customer friendly processes. Customer service is an integral part of our job and should not be seen as an extension of it.

A company's most vital asset is its customers. Without them, we would not and could not exist in business. When you satisfy our customers, they not only help us grow by continuing to do business with you, but recommend you to friends and associates. The practice of customer service should be as present on the show floor as it is in any other sales environment.

COMMANDMENTS OF CUSTOMER SERVICE

Know who is boss. You are in business to service customer needs, and you can only do that if you know what it is your customers want. When you truly listen to your customers, they let you know what they want and how you can provide good service. Never forget that the customer pays your salary and makes your job possible.

Be a Good Listener

Take the time to identify customer needs by asking questions and concentrating on what the customer is really saying. Listen to their words, tone of voice, body language, and most importantly, how they feel. Beware of making assumptions—thinking you intuitively know what the customer wants. Do you know what three things are most important to your customer?

Effective listening and undivided attention are particularly important on the show floor where there is a great danger of preoccupation—looking around to see to whom else we could be selling to. Identify and anticipate needs. Customers don't buy products or services. They buy good feelings and solutions to problems. Most customer needs are emotional rather than logical. The more you know your customers, the better you become at anticipating their needs. Communicate regularly so that you are aware of problems or upcoming needs.

Make customers feel important and appreciated. Treat them as individuals. Always use their name and find ways to compliment them, but be sincere. People value sincerity. It creates good feeling and trust. Think about ways to generate good feelings about doing business with you. Customers are very sensitive and know whether or not you really care about them. Thank them every time you get a chance.

On the show floor be sure that your body language conveys sincerity. Your words and actions should be congruent. Help customers understand your systems. Your organisation may have the world's best systems for getting things done, but if customers don't understand them, they can get confused, impatient and angry. Take time to explain how your systems work and how they simplify transactions. Be careful that your systems don't reduce the human element of your organisation.

Appreciate the power of "Yes". Always look for ways to help your customers. When they have a request (as long as it is reasonable) tell them that you can do it. Figure out how afterwards. Look for ways to make doing business with you easy. Always do what you say you are going to do.

Know How to Apologise

When something goes wrong, apologise. It's easy and customers like it. The customer may not always be right, but the customer must always win. Deal with problems immediately and let customers know what you have done. Make it simple for customers to complain. Value their complaints. As much as we dislike it, gives us an opportunity to improve. Even if customers are having a bad day, go out of your way to make them feel comfortable.

Give More than Expected

Since the future of all companies lies in keeping customers happy, think of ways to elevate yourself above the competition. Consider the following:

- What can you give customers that they cannot get elsewhere?
- What can you do to follow-up and thank people even when they don't buy?
- What can you give customers that is totally unexpected?

Get Regular Feedback

Encourage and welcome suggestions about how you could improve. There are several ways in which you can find out what customers think and feel about your services. There are as follows:

— Listen carefully to what they say.
— Check back regularly to see how things are going.
— Provide a method that invites constructive criticism, comments and suggestions.

Treat Employees Well

Employees are your internal customers and need a regular dose of appreciation. Thank them and find ways to let them know how important they are. Treat your employees with respect and chances are they will have a higher regard for customers. Appreciation stems from the top. Treating customers and employees well is equally important.

GOOD CUSTOMER SERVICE RULES

Good Customer Service Made Simple

Good customer service is the lifeblood of any business. You can offer promotions and slash prices to bring in as many new customers as you want, but unless you can get some of those customers to come back, your business won't be profitable for long.

Good customer service is all about bringing customers back. And about sending them away happy–happy enough to pass positive feedback about your business along to others, who may then try the product or service you offer for themselves and in their turn become repeat customers.

If you're a good salesperson, you can sell anything to anyone once. But it will be your approach to customer service that determines whether or not you'll ever be able to sell that person anything else. The essence of good customer service is forming a relationship with customers

—a relationship that individual customer feels that he would like to pursue.

How do you go about forming such a relationship? By remembering the one true secret of good customer service and acting accordingly; "You will be judged by what you do, not what you say." I know this verges on the kind of statement that's often seen on a sampler, but providing good customer service is a simple thing.

If you truly want to have good customer service, all you have to do is ensure that your business consistently does these things:

Answer Your Phone

Get call forwarding. Or an answering service. Hire staff if you need to. But make sure that someone is picking up the phone when someone calls your business.

Don't make Promises Unless you Will Keep them

Not plan to keep them. Will keep them. Reliability is one of the keys to any good relationship, and good customer service is no exception. If you say, "Your new bedroom furniture will be delivered on Tuesday", make sure it is delivered on Tuesday. Otherwise, don't say it. The same rule applies to client appointments, deadlines, etc.. Think before you give any promise – because nothing annoys customers more than a broken one.

Listen to Your Customers

Is there anything more exasperating than telling someone what you want or what your problem is and then discovering that person hasn't been paying attention and needs to have it explained again? From a customer's point of view, I doubt it. Can the sales pitches and the product babble. Let your customer talk and show him that you are listening by making the appropriate responses, such as suggesting how to solve the problem.

Deal with Complaints

No one likes hearing complaints, and many of us have developed a reflex shrug, saying, "You can't please all the people all the time". Maybe not, but if you give the complaint your attention, you may be able to please this one person this one time—and position your business to reap the benefits of good customer service.

Be Helpful

For example, one day John popped into a local watch shop because he had lost the small piece that clips the pieces of his watch band together. When he explained the problem, the proprietor said that he thought he might have one lying around. The proprietor found it, attached it to John's watch band – and charged him nothing!

Need Proper Training for your Staff

Do it yourself or hire someone to train them. Talk to them about good customer service and what it is (and isn't) regularly. Most importantly, give every member of your staff enough information and power to make those small customer-pleasing decisions, so he never has to say, "I don't know, but so-and-so will be back at..."

Take the Extra Step

Lead the customer to the item. Better yet, wait and see if he has questions about it, or further needs. Whatever the extra step may be, if you want to provide good customer service, take it. They may not say so to you, but people notice when people make an extra effort and will tell other people.

Throw in Something Extra

Whether it's a coupon for a future discount, additional information on how to use the product, or a genuine smile, people love to get more than they thought they were getting. And don't think that a gesture has to be large to be effective. The local art framer that we use attaches a package of picture hangers to every picture he frames. A small thing, but so appreciated. If you apply these eight simple rules consistently, your business will become known for its good customer service.

WAYS TO PROVIDE CUSTOMER SERVICE

Bring Them Back with Shiny Customer Service

There's no real secret to getting your customers to come back. All you need to do is provide customer service that exceeds your customers' expectations and outshines your competitors' customer service.

Acumen Research Group surveyed more than 1,000. In Canada, retail banking and telco customers to determine what made them behave loyally and what made them leave long-term relationships; 43 per cent of respondents abandoned a provider to which they declared themselves loyal because of a negative experience with a staff person, and 30 per cent of respondents reported that having the feeling they are not treated as valued customers by the staff has been the main reason for taking their business elsewhere.

Good customer service is service with a capital "S", Service that makes your customer feel special, Service that makes him or her want to come back and do more business with your company, and recommend your business to his or her friends. So how can you provide customer Service that shines? Follow this plan to ensure customer service that will dazzle customers and competitors alike:

Determine What Makes What you Offer Special

Study the competition. Think about their customer service and the customer service you provide. What can you offer your customers that is "better" than the competition? There are sure to be aspects of your customer Service that you can promote as "Special".

Make a list of all these ideas for providing customer service. If you sell a product, and your competitor doesn't offer it already, perhaps you can offer free local delivery. If you sell a service, such as bookkeeping or accounting, perhaps you can focus on turnaround times that are faster than your competitors'- providing the good customer service that will give your business the edge.

Sometimes providing customer Service that shines will involve expanding your operations. For instance, you may need to offer to provide your services in customer's homes to outdo the services the competition provides.

Sometimes providing customer Service that will involve revamping what you've always done. If you provide a service that involves giving estimates of the job to be done beforehand, and you've previously just given estimates to prospective customers orally, you could stress that you provide an estimate in writing and stick to your written estimate. Lower prices are not service; they're just lower prices.

Putting Your Customer Service Ideas into Action

Now that you have a list of customer service ideas that

you might use to provide customer service that outshines the customer service your competitors provide, it's time to look at implementing good customer service.

Study the Customer Service Ideas on Your List and Examine their Feasibility

Can you really guarantee that you will always stick to your written estimate or provide a faster turnaround time than your competitors? If you aren't sure, or can't do it, cross it off your customer service ideas list.

Choose one or Two of Your Good Customer Service Ideas and Implement them

Feature this aspect of your customer service in whatever ads you run, including your yellow pages listing. Put it on your business cards and in your email signature. Make it part of your greeting spiel when you answer the phone. You need to make your customer service a prominent feature of every ad too, so people automatically associate it with your business.

While one of the big pay-offs of your shiny customer service will be the great word-of-mouth advertising it generates, this takes time, and you need to help it along by getting the word out. Don't be shy! Solicit customer service testimonials from satisfied customers, that you can use in print ads, such as in newspapers, ezines, and on your website, if you have one, or can at least use as references for new potential customers.

Stay Proactive and Keep Gathering Customer Service Ideas

Listen to your customers and find out what kind of special customer service they want. You can do this formally, by creating a customer satisfaction feedback form that you enclose with every sale or post on your website, or informally, by asking them for their customer service ideas when they're in your store or office. Shiny customer service is service that's responsive to customers' needs.

Customers are tired of dealing with retailers that ignore customer service or only pretend to have it, and as always. A Customer Service Company will draw customers to your product or service, rather than a competitors', and bring them back in droves.

Good Customer Service is no Longer Enough

Your business would not exist without customers. And if you have customers, you have to have customer service. Today, there are so many companies who offers communication workshops and speeches in business and technical writing, proposal writing, customer service communications, interpersonal skills, resolving conflict, and more.

3

UNDERSTAND YOUR CUSTOMER

Customer needs may be defined as the goods or services a customer requires to achieve specific goals. Different needs are of varying importance to the customer. Customer's expectations are influenced by cultural values, advertising, marketing, and other communications, both with the supplier and with other sources.

Both customer needs and expectations may be determined through interviews, surveys, conversations, data mining or other methods of collecting information. Customers at times do not have a clear understanding of their needs. Assisting in determining needs can be a valuable service to the customer. In the process, expectations may be set or adjusted to correspond to known product capabilities or service.

In today's global business economy, technology advances have made the competitive landscape much tougher. Customers have access to more information and more avenues for service and purchase communication. And even though the Internet has stimulated competition, the same basic rules of business exist and survive. Satisfied customers will return to companies who provide good services and products.

Aside from the focus on quality offerings, companies now must also concentrate on how to interact with customers through personalised and intelligent transactions. Customer service differentiation will provide competitive advantages.

The cost of customer acquisition is far greater than the cost associated with customer retention. The Internet economy is no different. Competitors are just a click away, and e-customers know it. The e-business model does not differ greatly from traditional business models: both recognise the need to understand customer attributes, including loyalty, profitability, and opportunity.

The new economy simply requires that intelligent and automatic customer analysis can take the place of traditional human interactive analysis, when necessary, in order to complete massive numbers of successful transactions at Web speed. Companies that react quickly and interact with customers intelligently will take dominant market leadership positions.

Customer acquisition is based on offering the right products and services to the right groups of customers at the right time. Customer retention is based on customer satisfaction. Think Analytic that provides the foundation to really understand customers and build one-to-one relationships and personalised products and services based on customer needs.

TYPES OF CUSTOMERS

In the retail industry, it seems as though we are constantly faced with the issue of trying to find new customers. Most of us are obsessed with making sure our advertising, displays, and pricing all "scream out" to attract new customers. This focus on pursuing new customers is certainly prudent and necessary, but, at the same time, it can wind up hurting us. Therefore, our focus really should be on the 20 per cent of our clients who currently are our best customers.

In retail, this idea of focusing on the best current customers should be seen as an on-going opportunity. To better understand the rationale behind this theory and to face the challenge of building customer loyalty, we need to break down shoppers into five main types:

- *Loyal Customers*: They represent no more than 20 per cent of our customer base, but make up more than 50 per cent of our sales.
- *Discount Customers*: They shop our stores frequently, but make their decisions based on the size of our markdowns.
- *Impulse Customers*: They do not have buying a particular item at the top of their "To Do" list, but come into the store on a whim. They will purchase what seems good at the time.
- *Need-Based Customers*: They have a specific intention to buy a particular type of item.
- *Wandering Customers*: They have no specific need or desire in mind when they come into the store. Rather, they want a sense of experience and/or community.

If we are serious about growing our business, we need to focus our effort on the loyal customers, and merchandise our store to leverage the impulse shoppers. The other three types of customers do represent a segment of our business, but they can also cause us to misdirect our resources if we put too much emphasis on them.

Loyal Customers

Naturally, we need to be communicating with these customers on a regular basis by telephone, mail, email, etc. These people are the ones who can and should influence our buying and merchandising decisions. Nothing will make a Loyal Customer feel better than soliciting their input and showing them how much you value it. In my mind, you can never do enough for them. Many times, the more you do for them, the more they will recommend you to others.

Discount Customers

This category helps ensure your inventory is turning over and, as a result, it is a key contributor to cash flow. This same group, however, can often wind up costing you money because they are more inclined to return product.

Impulse Customers

Clearly, this is the segment of our clientele that we all like to serve. There is nothing more exciting than assisting an Impulse shopper and having them respond favourably to our recommendations. We want to target our displays towards this group because they will provide us with a significant amount of customer insight and knowledge.

Need-Based Customers

People in this category are driven by a specific need. When they enter the store, they will look to see if they can have that need filled quickly. If not, they will leave right away. They buy for a variety of reasons such as a specific occasion, a specific need, or an absolute price point. As difficult as it can be to satisfy these people, they can also become Loyal Customers if they are well taken care of. Sales people may not find them to be a lot of fun to serve, but, in the end, they can often represent your greatest source of long-term growth.

It is important to remember that Need-Based Customers can easily be lost to Internet sales or a different retailer. To overcome this threat, positive personal interaction is required, usually from one of your top salespeople. If they are treated to a level of service not available from the Web or another retail location, there is a very strong chance of making them Loyal Customers. For this reason, Need-Based Customers offer the greatest long-term potential, surpassing even the Impulse segment.

Wandering Customers

For many stores, this is the largest segment in terms of traffic, while, at the same time, they make up the smallest percentage of sales. There is not a whole lot you can do about this group because the number of Wanderers you have is driven more by your store location than anything else.

Keep in mind, however, that although they may not represent a large percentage of your immediate sales, they are a real voice for you in the community. Many Wanderers shop merely for the interaction and experience it provides them. Shopping is no different to them than it is for another person to go to the gym on a regular basis. Since they are merely looking for interaction, they are also very likely to communicate to others the experience they had in the store. Therefore, although Wandering Customers cannot be ignored, the time spent with them needs to be minimised.

Retail is an art, backed up by science. The science is the information we have from financial to research data (the "backroom stuff"). The art is in how we operate on the floor: our merchandising, our people, and, ultimately, our customers. For all of us, the competitive pressure has never been greater and it is only going to become more difficult. To be successful, it will require patience and understanding in knowing our customers and the behaviour patterns that drive their decision-making process.

Using this understanding to help turn Discount, Impulse, Need-Based, and even Wandering Customers into Loyal ones will help grow our business. At the same time, ensuring that our Loyal Customers have a positive experience each time they enter our store will only serve to increase our bottom-line profits.

WAYS OF UNDERSTANDING OUR CUSTOMERS

Buyer orientation—understanding and satisfying your customers—is essential for commercial success. Understanding one's customers is so important that large corporations spend hundreds of millions annually on market research. Although such formal research is important, a small firm can usually avoid this expense. Typically, the owner or manager of a small concern knows the customers personally. From this foundation, understanding of your customers can be built by a systematic effort. A comprehensive system for understanding is what Rudyard Kipling called his six honest serving men. "Their names are What and Why and When and How and Where and Who."

What

A seller characterises what customers are buying as goods and services - toothpaste, drills, video games cars. But understanding of buyers starts with the realisation that they purchase benefits as well as products. Consumers don't select toothpaste. Instead. some will pay for a decay preventive. Some seek pleasant taste. Others want bright teeth. Or perhaps any formula at a bargain price will do.

Similarly, industrial purchasing agents are not really interested in drills. They want holes. They insist on quality appropriate for their purposes, reliable delivery when needed, safe operation, and reasonable prices.

Video games are fun. They are bought for home entertainment, family togetherness, development of personal dexterity, introduction to computers, among other satisfactions. Commercial customers include arcades, pizza huts, and assorted enterprises. They benefit from a potential source of income, a means of attracting buyers to their premises, or perhaps a competitive move.

Similarly, cars are visible evidence of a person's wealth, reflection of life style, a private cabin for romance. Or they represent receipts from leases, means to pursue an occupation. Some people even buy cars for transportation.

You must find out, from their point of view, what customers are buying. The common names of products mean as little to them as the chemical names on the label of a proprietary drug. Understanding your customers enables you to profit by providing what buyers seeks - satisfaction.

Products change, but basic benefits like personal hygiene, attractiveness, safety, entertainment, and privacy endure. So do commercial purposes such as quests for competitive superiority or profitability.

Successful manufacturers and service establishments produce benefits for which customers are willing to pay. Successful wholesalers and retailers select offerings of such demanded benefits that they can resell at a profit. Successful business people, in other words. Understand the reason for their customers' buying decisions.

Why

The reason that customers buy is logical from their point

of view. Understanding customers derives from this fundamental premise. Don't argue with taste. Everybody is unique. Each person has individual pressures and criteria. Moreover, perceptions differ. The astute businessperson deduces and accepts the buying logic of customers and serves them accordingly.

To learn why customers buy can be quite difficult.

Some buyers hide their true motivations. In many cases the reasons are obscure to the buyers themselves. Most purchase decisions are multi-causal. Often, conflicts abound. A car buyer may want the roominess of a large vehicle and the fuel economy of a subcompact. The resolution of such mutually exclusive desires is usually indeterminate.

Sometimes the reasons why customers buy are trivial. If customers feel indifferent toward a product or store, the selection is apt to be happenstance. Perhaps several rival offerings meet all the conditions that a purchaser deems important. Consequently, minor factors govern. This explains the rationale of the consumer who chose a Rs. 12 lacks car because its upholstery was most attractive. The point: Pay attention to details. They may be crucial to customers.

Often the best clues are the customers' actions. Shrewd business people respect what people say, but pay special attention to what people do. More important than why customers buy is why former customers have taken their patronage elsewhere and why qualified buyers are not buying. What is now keeping them from buying?

Can this obstacle be surmounted? Business people monitor competitive offerings and buyers' reactions to infer clues. Informal conversations may also reveal some reasons. Special offers may overcome resistance and boost profits.

All the time the manager must be careful to retain the company's regular customers. For instance, a specialty dress shop may try to widen its patronage through a new line at bargain prices. This move could disturb the store's usual patrons. They may take their trade to another store that caters exclusively to their social class.

Many of the dresses were bought for special occasions when projection of a genteel image was important to the customer. Understanding of customers includes awareness of the time of the purchase and use of the merchandise.

When

A seller must be ready when the buyer is, lest an opportunity be irretrievably lost. Customers buy when they want an offering and have the time and money to purchase it. Buying patterns can often be discerned from an analysis of customers and their purchases. For example, wants for many consumer goods and services are tied to customers' rites of passage. The following purchase occasions in the adult life cycle are typical:

— Marriage, separation, divorce

— Acquisition of a home

— Change in employment or career

— Graduate study

— Health care, injury, illness

— Pregnancy, nurture of children

— Children enter school; graduate

— Children leave home (for college or permanently)

— Move to another area

— Vacations; major social activities

— Permanent retirement from work

— Death of a family member.

Shrewd retailers keep track of such key buying events and gain a head start on making sales. Logs of birthdays and anniversaries are a case in point. Additional purchase occasions are impersonal. Seasonal factors include recurring holidays and weather changes. Among other favourable influences on purchases are start of the school year, semiannual white sales, introduction of new models and clearance of old ones, special price concessions, and improvement in economic conditions or buyer's confidence.

Some of the latter factors also apply to manufacturers. Small plants work closely with their buyers' inventory managers and replenish stock at their reorder point. A current vogue is just-in-time delivery. Interactive computers make replenishment notices routine.

Many consumers have time for shopping only during off hours. In the evenings, and on weekends. The trend from a single breadwinner per family toward having all adults of a household engage in commercial employment has intensified this time peculiarity. Astute retailers adjust their hours, staffing, and availability of merchandise to customers' shopping convenience. Bartenders know that business booms on payday. Manufacturers profit from timing their offers to their customers' budgetary cycles. Thus, knowing when products are bought and used is a valuable facet of understanding customers.

Although a transaction may be concluded in a moment, most purchases actually entail a drawn-out process. This process will be described in the next section which analyses how customers buy.

How

Knowledge of how customers buy pays off in several ways. (1) Sellers can design their offerings to meet the exact needs of their buyers. (2) Sellers can influence decision makers at crucial steps of the buying process. (3) Sellers can lay the groundwork for repeat business.

Buying methods are best visualised as processes. Household purchases usually start when a consumer has a desire or a problem that an acquisition might satisfy or solve. Industrial purchases usually start when a user or a routine sets off a signal (requisition) for approval of a procurement.

People are diverse. Every consumer, every firm pursues a buying process of its own. Buying processes also depend on the significance of the product to the buyer and on other circumstances. Although buying processes are not uniform. Some steps are common to most of them. The seller needs to know only these critical steps when he or she can affect the outcome of the buying decision.

Shrewd sellers delve into the behavioural milestones of purchasers. But for each very important customer the buying process should be diagrammed individually, showing names of influencers at each decision stage, elapsed time between stages, and any other pertinent information.

Perhaps a change in life-style or a demonstration at a friend's house has caused this consumer to recognise the need for a personal computer. But lack of knowledge and the fear of a wrong decision may counteract this desire. The process continues, however, if advertisements and expected benefits persuade the consumer to act. Despite budgetary constraints and uncertainty about future needs, the consumer proceeds to compare stores and brands.

At this search and evaluation stage advice from present satisfied customers is especially influential. Make sure your customers are satisfied and favourably recommend your merchandise or service. To the contrary, poor shopping facilities or irritating personnel can sway the potential customer against making the purchase from you.

Sooner or later, further search does not seem worthwhile. If the positives still outweigh the negatives, the consumer picks a store and brand. The transaction itself is consummated quickly, assuming the wanted item is available. The satisfied customer makes recommendations to others and gives you his or her repeated, regular business.

Business people can create sales by predisposing potential buyers to their product or store. Manufacturers can offer exclusive benefits in their goods, such as friendly relations, efficient operations, and easy manuals. Enticing advertisements help persuade prospects to visit a retail outlet and ask about a particular brand. Creative salespeople overcome the customer's objections and doubts and close the sale. Post-transaction service keeps the customer satisfied. Referrals usually follow.

Specific details are needed to track acquisition of something complex, say a computer. On the other hand, less detail is needed if the purchase is laundry detergent or some other staple with which the customer is less involved. In the latter case, depletion of the home inventory triggers a routine, leading directly to choice: the usually purchased brand. If the usual brand is out-of-stock or another brand is on sale. A substitute may be bought quickly. Brand comparisons follow or may be omitted.

Some products are bought when an emergency need for them arises. A physical examination and the filling of a prescription are urgent when sickness strikes. Arrangements for funerals follow immediately after the death of a family member. Umbrellas are in demand when it rains. An unexpected snow storm generates extra calls for tire chains, towing services, and car batteries. Often, convenient availability determines when these goods and services are purchased. And even if customers do have ample time to select merchandise, sellers who stand ready to supply wanted or expected brands are apt to gain preference and profit when shoppers decide where to buy.

People want options. Although convenient availability is the main buying criterion for many routine household products, savvy merchants stock a selection conforming to the diverse preferences of their patrons. Some people demand manufacturers' advertised brands. Resellers' brands are favoured by others. On some classes of goods, generic brands have become popular in recent years. Moreover, many consumers seek occasional variety. Clearly the decision of which products to stock is important.

It is more important yet on shopping goods because buyers compare them before purchase. And it is most important on specialty goods, those preselected by brand name. If a store does not stock these uniquely wanted brands, a prospect will leave without buying. Whoever offers them on acceptable terms gains the sale.

Where

From a multitude of studies emerge different criteria for deciding where to shop. Most research on the subject agrees that store location is a major consideration, Stores usually draw most of their patronage from their surrounding neighbourhood.

Savvy store managers make a special effort to understand the shopping-related motivations and preferences of local residents. New managers of fast-food units, for example, canvass nearby dwellings and introduce themselves to the households. Some supermarkets maintain consumer advisory boards to elicit suggestions and reactions. Other means of communication with customers include informal conversations at the store and suggestion boxes with interviews and awards.

Incidentally, complaints are an excellent guide for making store policies more amenable to customers. Personnel should be instructed to thank patrons for their comments. Prompt consideration, followed by a personal letter from the store manager, is highly desirable.

Location is extremely important to "captive" buyers. Exclusively franchised utilities, shops in isolated hotels. and cafeterias or automatic vending machines in factories are examples. At the opposite extreme, shoppers escape spatial restrictions by buying from mail-order firms or telephone solicitors.

Other patronage influences vary. They depend on the type of product. Type of store, and the characteristics of the consumer. The offered assortment's perceived quality. Depth, and breadth certainly are very important. Along with price, This does not imply that all goods have to be top quality or all prices the lowest. Perceptions are decisive.

If quality seems high, some customers infer that prices are high too regardless of the facts. The important point is to understand customers and to provide what causes them to buy. For example, assurance of repair service weighs heavily with the worrier type of customer. A convenience-minded buyer is concerned with parking space or delivery service.

Of course, shoppers must be told that wanted goods and services are available. Advertising helps disseminate this information. So does a store's reputation for consistent policies of satisfying its customers. Occasional promotions inject some excitement into the tedium of shopping. Some clients like to socialise, which can absorb much of an employee's time and may even annoy other buyers. Nevertheless, personnel should be friendly and helpful. Also influential, for some customers, is the apparent socioeconomic level of other shoppers.

Personal affinity for other customers or for salespeople is a decisive factor in the success of party-selling, e.g., household goods and in-home selling (cosmetics). The choice of where to buy items requiring major outlays (securities, and insurance) often revolves around from whom to buy.

In selecting a retail store, many customers consider physical features. Layouts can invite or repel patronage. Motorists who are in a hurry, for instance, are apt to use a petrol pump at which business can be transacted quickly. Altogether, buyers perceive a mix of tangible and intangible factors that comprise a store's atmosphere. Accordingly, they either do or don't feel comfortable about shopping there.

To the casual observer, all supermarkets seem more or Hess alike, But. in fact, store managers can regulate many of the above-mentioned variables and thereby affect where shoppers buy. According to recent studies in several American cities, household buyers perceive supermarkets in their neighbourhood as sufficiently different to determine their patronage preference. The four main types of supermarkets offer: (1) High quality at commensurate prices, (2) Lowest price level in the area, (3) Swift completion, (4) Friendly atmosphere. Each can profit by appealing to a different segment of buyers. The topic of the next section.

Who

Identification of customers and prospects makes effective targeting possible. Small business owners pride themselves on knowing their customers personally. In the industrial field, understanding of each major customer and buying influence is essential. When dealing with a large number of customers, however, individual familiarity is not feasible. Hence mass merchandisers and others in this situation group their customers, whose reactions to offerings are similar, into segments. Then they design a separate appropriate marketing programme for each segment.

Strategies vary, A small firm might prosper by concentrating its resources on one segment. Because customers are volatile, the specialising firm is vulnerable to sudden change in its target segment's patronage. Hence some companies address several segments simultaneously. Although expensive, a strategy of employing different tactics for different segments can be quite profitable. Other firms scatter offers to just anybody. They hope that segments will select themselves.

One basis for segmentation is geographic. Retail customers are apt to live or work in the store's vicinity. Industrial buyers tend to concentrate regionally. So do users of services. Intensive cultivation of local potential customers can be efficient and lucrative. Personal knowledge of local buyers and a shared community spirit help cement relations with these customers.

Segmentation is an art. All "honest serving men"—what, why, when, how, where, as well as who—can be the key to segmentation. Whatever the basis, each identified segment should have sufficient purchasing power to make a special effort commercially worthwhile. Accessibility is vital. How can the segment be reached? Are advertisements, telephone solicitations, or personal visits efficient? How about trade shows or personal contacts? The ideal segment is stable in purchase needs and loyalty, helping you fend off competition.

Besides segmentation, understanding of customers also requires insight into their buying roles. The buyer for a one-person household or one-person business is the initiator of the order, the decider, and the user. Even in this case, however, some outsiders are influential.

In larger households or businesses, these buying roles are usually played by separate individuals. It helps you to know who activates (requisitions) purchases, who exerts influence, who decides what and where to buy, who uses the product-and what their criteria are. Then you tailor and target your offerings to satisfy each major participant in the buying process.

As has been shown, understanding of customers enables a seller to increase sales. This same understanding can equally serve to reduce costs. Higher sales at lower costs inevitably boost profits. A small firm that understands its customers can buy or produce exactly what they want-and nothing else. The firm's sales effort is efficient because it builds on why its customers want to buy not on why others buy, or why the vendor wants to sell.

Merchandise can be ready when customers need it. Thus a knowledgeable seller avoids unnecessary inventory costs or penalties for late delivery. Understanding how customers buy lets a seller employ promotional media, appeals, and timing for maximum effectiveness. Transportation costs are lowered by shipping merchandise to where it is needed. Knowledge of who comprises suitable segments and the separate buying roles can reduce the waste of soliciting unqualified or uninterested people.

CUSTOMERS ARE DYNAMIC

The best source for you to learn about customers is your personal interaction with them. At work, social and civic activities, and chance encounters, people talk and reveal their attitudes and motivation. Listen to your customers. You can also keep abreast of purchasing patterns by observing competitors' practices and by asking sales personnel who is buying what, where.

Understanding Your Customers Through their Own Stories

Many organisations could be wasting scarce resources on unnecessary customer research when there are cheaper and far more effective solutions. There is a danger of using research as a safety net, validating common-sense decisions and supplying relatively obvious information about what customers think and feel.

Some marketers now seem to delegate responsibility for thinking and decision-making to research companies. Yet much of the customer intelligence in these research debriefs already exists within organisations—and in a format that is easier to understand and remember, and is far more engaging, than Power Point presentations or documents. It also encourages innovative solutions.

Such customer intelligence exists in the form of customer stories, which can replace the safety net of customer research. They can be a springboard for customer-based innovation. Stories about your customers are everywhere in your organisation, in the chitchat in the lunchroom, in emails, at the coffee machine. Such stories are easy to tap into, and collectively they can increase the levels of customer understanding, insight and creativity in the organisation, without expensive research.

Tapping Into the Power of Customer Stories

So how can you collect these customer stories? Following are some tips:

— Employees that interact directly with customers can use notebooks to write down interesting customer stories as they happen. These can be collected and collated regularly.

— Listen in to call centre calls. They are a rich source of customer stories.

— Try cheap and easy ways to get stories from your customers, such as surveys and questionnaires. Don't worry about the expense of statistically significant approaches or expensive questionnaire design.

— Leverage the Web. There is far more talk about your organisation on the web than you could ever imagine. It's happening now, in chat rooms, special interest groups, consumer Web sites and competitive Web sites.

Bringing Your Customers to Life

Of course, once you have all this rich insight into your customers, the challenge is how to apply it. How can you get inside the head of your customers every time you need to make a decision? Borrow a few fiction-writing techniques:

— Turn your existing customer segments into real people, by giving them distinguishing characteristics: names, looks, clothes, hobbies, secrets, hopes and fears.

— Be sure to give your customer segments a life outside their role as your customer. One way of creating a character from your existing data is by stealing characteristics from your friends and family. If someone you know seems to fit what you know about a particular customer segment, you can add their characteristics to the picture you create.

— Judge ideas and make decisions by testing them against your customer characters. Some writers have imaginary conversations with their characters to help them decide what they should do. You can do the same. Some marketing people imagine their different customers sitting in empty chairs and talk to them, to help them make decisions. No, they are not mad, and it does work!

— Give your different customer characters different "anchors." An anchor is a stimulus that allows you to slip into the right frame of mind for a different customer character. You decide what it is. Some writers choose different pieces of music, words or picture that represents some aspect of their character.

All of these techniques bring your customers to life, allowing you to make better decisions, based on a more complete customer understanding. These techniques remove the time and expense of research, improve the levels of customer understanding in your organisation, and encourage innovative thinking.

4

CUSTOMER RELATIONSHIP MANAGEMENT

Customer Relationship Management (CRM) is the practice of intelligently finding, marketing to, selling to, and servicing customers. There are three aspects of CRM which can each be implemented in isolation from each other:

1. *Operational*: Automation of customer processes that offers support to a company's sales or service representative.
2. *Collaborative*: The programme communicates to customers without a company's sales or service representative.
3. *Analytical*: Analysis of customer information for multiple purposes.

OPERATIONAL CRM

Operational CRM provides support to "front office" business processes, including sales, marketing and service. Each interaction with a customer is generally added to a customer's contact history, and staff can retrieve information on customers from the database when necessary. One of the main benefits of this contact history is that customers can interact with different people or different contact *channels* in a company over time without having to describe the history of their interaction each time. Consequently, many call centers use some kind of CRM software to support their call center agents. Operational CRM process customer data for a variety of purposes:

1. Managing campaigns.
2. Enterprise marketing automation.
3. Sales force automation.

COLLABORATIVE CRM

The function of the customer interaction system or collaborative customer relationship management is to collaborate the multi-channel service and support given to the customer; providing the infrastructure for responsive and effective support to customer issues, questions complaints etc.

ANALYTICAL CRM

Analytical CRM analyses customer data for a variety of purposes:

— Design and execution of targeted marketing campaigns to optimise-marketing effectiveness.

— Design and execution of specific customer campaigns, including customer acquisition, cross-selling, up-selling, retention.

— Analysis of customer behaviour to aid product and service decision making.

— Management decisions, e.g. financial forecasting and customer profitability analysis.

— Prediction of the probability of customer defection.

CRM STRATEGY

Several commercial CRM software packages are available which vary in their approach to CRM. However, CRM is not just a technology, but rather a comprehensive approach to an organisation's philosophy in dealing with its customers. This includes policies and processes, front-of-house customer service, employee training, marketing, systems and information management. Hence, it is important that any CRM implementation considerations stretch beyond technology, towards the broader organisational requirements.

The objectives of a CRM strategy must consider a company's specific situation and its customers needs and expectations. CRM strategies can vary in size, complexity and scope. Some companies consider a CRM strategy to only focus on the management of a team of salespeople. However, other CRM strategies can cover customer interaction across the entire organisation. Many commercial CRM software packages that are available provide features that serve sales, marketing, event management, project management and finance.

One of the primary functions of CRM software is to collect information about customers. Therefore, the data gathered as part of CRM solution must consider customer privacy and data security with respect to legal and cultural environments. Some customers prefer assurance that their data is not shared with third parties without their consent and not accessed illegally by third parties.

Customers can benefit from their data being utilised within a CRM system. For instance, an increase in unsolicited telemarketing calls is generally resented by customers while a small number of relevant offers is generally appreciated by customers. CRM software can enhance the collection and analysis of customer behaviour leading to more relevant communications with customers.

LESSONS FOR CRM

There are five lessons you have learned over the years about customer relationship management that have both helped reduce the tension and build confidence in your customers.

1. Call the Customer

When things go wrong and the customer knows, call. Email does not always translate circumstances or feelings well as there is no voice inflection and a customer usually places more value on a phone call. Discuss the situation and have solutions ready! Also have a time line ready for implementing the solutions and resolving the problems. Be sure you can deliver on the timeline; this will restore confidence. People in crises situations feel less stress when they know what to expect. When you execute the solutions and the customer is aware of this they will increase their confidence in you and relax more.

2. Keep the Customer Informed

When things go wrong and the customer doesn't know, it is still a good idea to let them know. The majority of the time your customer will find out about the problem anyway.

3. Offer Solutions

Have solutions ready for customers when there are problems. Do not expect them to tell you what to do. Offer them solutions and ask for their thoughts. In my case customers have most often said, "What do you think we should do?" This shows the customer that you have thought about the problem and have it under control.

4. Watch those Promises

Do not promise what you cannot deliver. It is always better to "under promise and over deliver" as they say. This is critical in the above scenarios and always true with customers. Set realistic timelines and budgets and add a little padding so you can absolutely deliver what you promised and then some. This will pay off in spades. Customers will be more likely to refer you and more likely to use you in the future.

5. Add Value

Add value to you and your business by bringing the customer ideas. For example, you might make these suggestions to a Web site customer: "Have you ever thought of using Google Adsense to add a revenue stream to your site? I noticed that your site is not in the Open Directory Project; have you considered submitting it? Do you have a tracking system on your site? I have found this is a good way to understand where people are entering your site and where they might be leaving, as a tracking system may offer insights into navigation problems which lead to audience attrition. New pitches, marketing strategies, anything that is of value that will help move the customer's business forward will be appreciated. The drawback comes when a customer starts spending a lot of your time talking about new ideas. It is important to be careful with this one. Be sure that the relationship is set up so everyone respects one another's time.

USING KNOWLEDGE MANAGEMENT FOR CRM

We live in an increasingly service-oriented economy. A better phrase might be an "attention-oriented economy". No doubt you already understand the importance of serving your customers well in order to retain their repeat business and referrals. However, the key factor that seems to be misunderstood is applying the knowledge each of your employees has in order to develop relationships with your clients. From building trust and rapport with clients to making yourself an expert at what you do, the power of knowledge can propel you ahead of your competition. Below are a few areas in which managing your knowledge can help you improve customer relations and customer service efforts:

Create a Collective Database

By using simple software you can create a basic knowledge management programme that revolves around the availability of customer information.

Have all the information about your customers in one place. Allow information such as conversations, likes and dislikes, birthdays, important dates, preferred shipping methods and any special considerations regarding the company. When you collect such information and store it for ready access you are equipping your employees to respond quickly and consistently to customer demands. Companies that use these kinds of knowledge management tools save thousands of dollars and at the same improve their customer service ratings.

Sun Microsystems, a multi-million-dollar corporation in California, USA, implemented such a programme and estimated that their sales and marketing force saved millions of dollars in training new hires alone. Sales people had all the information they needed in order to provide for customers. Because each person within the organisation participated in adding database information, a complete picture of the customer was obtained.

Solve Customer Problems

Get into the routine of bringing up client information as soon as you establish contact. By having your customer's past history right in front of you, will be in a better position to assist them. By understanding the particulars of your customer's business you will be able to offer assistance and recommend your organisation's products/ services. You might find your customer complaining of difficulties in a specific area and be able to suggest they try a new product your business is offering. By showing that you have the ability to access and use information dealing with past orders, an organisational profile or other helpful information, you are proving to your client that service comes first.

Improve Your Processes

Create a special field and instruct each employee to input even the smallest complaint into the database. Once a month (or quarter) review the complaints to see how you might improve upon your own processes and policies in order to be more customer-friendly.

How many times have you called an organisation and had to enter your account number or telephone number once the automated attendant answered? Then, after being greeted by a company representative, you were asked again for the same information you had already provided. This is an irritant for most people. By collecting information regarding the complaints of your customers, you will be able to overcome such inefficiencies.

The most serious complaint regarding customer service is that corporations are perceived as being uncaring. This simple knowledge management effort will greatly increase the perception that you do value your clients.

The more you know about your customers and their needs, the better you will be able to serve them. You will be able to design products that will solve problems. You will be equipped to improve and adjust your services to be more customer-oriented. But most importantly, you will create an environment where each customer feels as if they are being shown preferential treatment.

Starting a KM Initiative

In organisational settings, knowledge is equal to the intellectual capital; your people's knowledge—what they know, your intellectual properties, etc. If you don't have a good knowledge management system in place, your best investment is walking out the door! Knowledge is not about having the brightest brains in your company, it's about leveraging them correctly. It is simply about putting to use what your people know and getting them to share what they know.

Knowledge Management (KM) was formally born the last decade because of the need to managing the lost knowledge of the workers who lost their job or left the company. Anytime there is turnover, regardless of the reason, it leaves a hole. This is why corporations struggle while trying to fill a job opening. When the employee left, so did the knowledge.

Effective knowledge management is empowerment for the intelligent organisation. Imagine being able to collectively share the intellect and the experiences of all your working people. It gives you the advantage of addressing your competition on the basis of what they know- simply it gives you a new strategic advantage.

When you have an organisation where you are able to reuse customer solutions, when you are able to utilise knowledge for daily operations, integrate knowledge from other knowledge workers to your own—all this will enable you to be more competitive.

Below are a few basics you need to have in place prior of starting a KM initiative. Implementing these first will help ensure success for your new programme.

— *First, you need to be motivated and inspired by this new process*—Consider the implementation of a KM programme as a "lifestyle change". This is not a one-time deal where consultants come in, pitch you about the new programme and leave. KM needs to be part of your organisational culture—an integrated philosophy of how you are doing business.

— *Get closer to your customer*—The more you know about your customers the better you will be able to serve them. What information do they need you to provide? Can you provide it in a timely and effective manner? Do your employees have access to the information they need to serve your customers well?

— *Give your teams permission to explore the new process*—You will need to allow team members time to explore and become familiar with this process. This can be as simple as arranging temporary "visitation" in other departments. A simple, one-day visit to each department within the organisation can provide an entirely new understanding of what is available to them. In reality, you can not force anyone to share their knowledge, but what you can do is expose them to an environment where they will be able to get to know each other on a personal level. After this, the information flow will open wide.

— *Provide your people with the technical resources*—Without the technology in place it will be very difficult to have a true KM environment. There are many wonderful KM programmes out in the market. If your company is interested in acquiring one of these, you can view several KM vendors by visiting a trusted website. One inexpensive and effective intelligence system can be created by integrating your email system with a database programme.

— *Built knowledge networks*—Support the formation of groups and communities. Create a network of people within your organisation. Networking communities is the best way of creating true KM environments. By encouraging employees to communicate among themselves you are in fact developing human databases. The cross training or knowledge sharing effect naturally emerges.

— *Integrate your knowledge sharing work with your business strategy*—Making decisions without gathering complete data from each and every department is dangerous. Don't assume any longer. The knowledge transfer must reach from entry-level employees all the way to the top. The executives that decide about next year's objectives need to know and be aware of everything that goes on at every level. An effective KM programme can make this insurmountable task manageable.

A KM programme is not something that only allows organisations to collect knowledge. This is a programme that benefits employees and customers alike. Work becomes more productive and fun, frustration diminishes because information is readily available, employee retention increases due to improved job satisfaction and customer satisfaction rates increase also.

Knowledge Management Strategy

Strategy development and actual strategy implementation has always been a challenge for organisations.

Mainly because the people that set up the strategy have so little to do with the actual implementation and there is not enough input, involvement from the actual implementation people. They know their customers inside out, yet they have little say when it comes to what the customers may want to see from the company in the year to come.

The solution is simple, yet it is on of these remedies that we know what is good for us, however we fail to follow through. In any case the benefits of involving all parties to contribute to a strategy are tremendous, companies will not only be able to foresee problems, that they were not able to see through by themselves but they will also gain commitment and loyalty from their employees. And if you think that the voices of the implementation folks are heart through their bosses and bosses, just remember the Arabic telephone. How accurate is the information that is going to be delivered to the board of directors? Would it hurt to include people with a variety of roles across the organisation? Does it have to be only the say of few powerful that are most likely saying the same things anyway?

There have been many attempts to solve this issue in the past decade, with many initiatives that took place, such as the Management by Objective wave yet, these initiatives faint away as time passes and still the inclusion of important people to a business strategy seems to be a problem.

The missing link between strategy development and strategy implementation becomes obvious and demands for an immediate remedy, in today's need for implementing Knowledge Management initiatives. Companies are heavily investing millions of dollars in knowledge management software, hardware and technical training so that these mediums (means) can actually preserve and harvest some of the organisational knowledge. Their hope is to store organisational knowledge in large depositories and make it available to their entire organisation. The real question comes, How are companies making sure that they need to integrate their business strategy with knowledge management strategy and make sure that the implementation folks will actually be there to Well, how does this work?

Revolutionary companies across the world have begun to develop a new set of processes for coaching people on how to contribute to a business strategy. There are a lot of case studies about these companies and a great deal of information can be learnt of them.

How can companies make sure that everyone is contributing to a business strategy or better a knowledge strategy, let's assume that the company decided to merge its knowledge strategy with its business strategy. Below are few helpful tips that illustrate how this is possible.

First, goals are set with the whole group in mind, remember our implementation people, well they get the privilege of having an actually say when it comes to setting the strategy for next year. Open discussion is encouraged and people seem not to be afraid to express their opinion.

Second, the whole plan is not focused only on results. It also focuses on why they want to achieve the results that they want to achieve? How is there vision going to add value to their customer base? And also what are the means and methods for achieving this vision? The actual resources that they are going to use or engage for setting and executing the strategy.

Third, everyone understands that the environment is constantly changing; therefore they are not in love with their first strategy. Strategies need to have room for flexibility and this is not difficult once you know your purpose of engaging in that strategy in the first place. That's why it is so clear to know the WHY you are doing anything? What is the ultimate result that you are seeking form it?

Fourth, constructive feedback is encouraged and actually recommendation are immediately implemented or included for future planning.

Fifth, these knowledge companies focus a lot on personal development and growth they understand that only then companies can actually be able to engage everyone in a strategy when people are acknowledged through the entire year not only for one day. You cannot expect people will want to work for you and contribute their best if you do not do your part.

As a corporate employer, you will need to be able to see that each person within your company has the capacity of adding value to your corporate strategy. The real challenge here is to have all these people work for your strategy for the entire year. Their voices need to heart, valued and actually given credit for. This is a radical strategically breakthrough but it is needed if you want to engage your whole company in contributing to your knowledge- business strategy.

E-BUSINESS AND CRM

Using the internet and e-business to provide products and services and information to customers require that you really know and understand your customers' needs. When customers contact your traditional business by visiting the store or office or contacting someone personally by phone, you have the opportunity to hear their questions and offer solutions based on personal communication. If they have a misunderstanding about your product or a sales objection you can deal with it immediately. When people visit your online business at your website, you will not even know they are there. You do not have the opportunity to ask or answer questions. It is therefore vitally important that you anticipate their questions and concerns and provide the needed information in a way that makes it easy for them to fully understand your offering. Customer Relationship Management (CRM) is a way to get the maximum value from your e-business investment.

CRM is the broad category of concepts, tools, and processes that allows an organisation to understand and serve everyone with whom it comes into contact. CRM is about gathering information that is used to serve customers-basic information, such as name, address, meeting and purchase history, and service and support contacts. In a supplier relationship it might be procurement history, terms and conditions, or contact information. This information is then used to better serve the clients.

Customers need to be able to find out about your products and services and be able to make purchases. You need to track each customer's activity in order to make offers of complimentary products and new products that you may provide. Keeping in mind that eighty per cent of your business will come from twenty per cent of your customers—the 80/20 principle—it will be important for you to know who is among the twenty per cent when they visit your site.

Investors will have needs that relate to the operation of the business and the performance of their investment. Making some of that information available on the web site will accomplish two things:

1. Investors will be better informed, and they will be able to find out the information they require without making specific inquires that take time to provide;

2. Investors will get the same information at the same time.

Suppliers and partners want to be connected with your organisation. Creating special places where these strategic partners can participate is valuable. Providing them with information, such as product promotions, press releases, and advertising campaigns will build strong relationships.

Needs of Online Customers

Online customers are different from those who are able to contact you and deal with you directly. They have a unique set of expectations. Generally, they expect immediate service, either by finding what they need on your site themselves; or, they may expect that the goods or services be delivered without delay. It is also common for prospective customers to have new or different levels of understanding about your business. An example of this was found by a book printing company that moved to the web to deliver a new "print to need" service.

Their existing customers are those organisations and individuals that have books and manuscripts ready to print and simply required final printing service. What they found was that individuals with books in progress or even those with the idea that they might want to write a book were now visiting their site. These potential customers need information about the self-publishing process before they are ready to buy services. It is important to provide information services to satisfy their requirements, so they will use the book printing services when they're ready.

Those organisations that understand the opportunity to build community on the Internet will be successful. A great example of this is an Alberta-based producer of specialty flower bulbs. This company began building its web presence by learning where its customers "hung out" on the web. They discovered their customers visited other flower-related sites and gardening portals, associated chat groups, and online forums. Therefore, the company spent time establishing links and alliances with these other sites to attract customers to its site.

The company recognised early on that they did not seek a technology solution, but rather a solution that provided a place for flower lovers to find new and unique products. As a result, they have attracted customers from all over North America and are making inroads into Asia. They also have seen another significant benefit-their average order size has increased by almost seven times. When people find their site and decide to place an order, orders are large.

The concept of community is also illustrated by the success of e-businesses like EBay, where specialty products are auctioned as well as more common products. People interested in antiques and collectibles have "gathered" at E-Bay to buy and sell.

Portals, those sites that act as anchors, start sites, or comprehensive market-oriented locations have also discovered the power of community. A site like Agriplace.com is one where those who are interested in agriculture can find just about everything related to this industry. News, references, product information and the ability to buy and sell related products are all available on the site.

Managing Customer Relations

It takes ten times more effort and costs ten times more money to attract a new customer than to keep an existing customer. This "statistic" alone should be enough for companies to invest in CRM. Finding customers is the first step and the faster you get through the sorting process of qualifying prospects into customers, the faster will be the returns. A web environment adds to this process in a very positive way. You can provide the means for people visiting your site to select whether they are indeed right to be customers. Good design and clear information will aid in this goal.

Finding the Customer

The process starts with finding customers. The Internet allows you to attract customers in two ways:

1. Getting them to find you through search engines, links, and alliances with other sites; and
2. By proactively finding them and sending material electronically.

The number one way people find online businesses is through search engines. There are a number of general-purpose engines where you can be registered, such as Altavista, Google, Yahoo!, and MSN. Because each of the major engines works differently in the way they index information, it is advised that companies engage a person or company that has experience in this activity.

A knowledgeable service provider will provide you with prominent placement in the searches. Whether you are in the oil and gas, tourism, or agriculture industries, there are search engines that specialise in information focused on these markets. It is also valuable to have your site linked from other complimentary e-businesses. Find web sites that your prospective customers visit, and then request a link to your site.

Building Value for the Customer

Now that you have found your customer, it is important to find ways to add value to the relationship. Keep in mind that value is in the mind of the customer. Find out what they perceive to be valuable by surveying them either online, by phone, or by regular mail. Even though you are using online techniques, do not forget the many other ways to connect with customers.

One very successful software company allows prospective customers to register at their web site, download an industry related document, and then phones the prospect within two hours to make sure they received the information successfully. This technique provides a further opportunity to get to know the customer and build the relationship. Afterwards, the company follows up with a letter.

Another way to add value is to produce newsletters that can be delivered online or by mail. Newsletters can be related to product or service announcements and contain general industry information. E-newsletters are simple and inexpensive to produce and deliver. A good rule of thumb is to keep the newsletter small and to discuss only two or three concepts.

As you build the relationship with your online customer you will be able to solicit and build more profile information. Information about product preferences allows you to offer complimentary products or give specials on items of interest to a specific set of customers.

Establishing Long-Term Relationships

As you gain more experience with online services you might use more sophisticated ways to build customer loyalty and strong relationships. Building customised or personalised sites for your customers to use will provide both added services and give customers a reason to return regularly to your e-business. You can see examples of personalised sites at many of the portals listed in the reference material.

E-Loyalty

It is easy to get customers to visit your website for the first time. It is much more difficult to get them to return. You must create value for the return visitor. Ensuring you have good content can do this. Content can be unique articles about the industry or simply links to other sources of information. Content can also be tools that a visitor may find useful. Many real estate sites have mortgage calculators or home buying checklists that aid customers in using the service. Acknowledging the purchasing history of a customer and thanking them for the business when they return to the site can earn loyalty. One way to have customers return is to provide incentives for the second or subsequent purchases.

Customer Experience at the Web Site

The first thing to get right is the creation of a web site that is easy for your visitors to use. It needs to be clear, concise, and include content that is appropriate for your visitor's needs. Understanding your customers' technology characteristics, including the type of hardware, software and connections they are likely to have, helps in the design of the site. If your customers are likely to have low-speed, dial-up connections, they will not be able to handle the more advanced features of some web creation systems.

A site that is easy to navigate will be more valuable to your visitors. Adding a site map and using clearly marked buttons can improve navigation. Put yourself in the place of your customer visiting your site. You know what your site does and the "jargon" that might be on the site, but does your customer? Most web site failures are a result of making assumptions about what the customers want, rather than really knowing.

FAQs

You can anticipate the questions that customers might have and put the questions and responses in an area known as a FAQ. Simple implementations will allow visitors to scroll through the list with more advanced sites, adding keyword search capability and at the high end, you can set up a system where clients e-mail questions, when they do not find the answer they are looking for. Afterwards the answer is automatically added to the FAQ list.

Real-Time Service Chat

By using products like Live Person from liveperson.com or Webex Oncall from webex.com, you can deliver personal services either as a text-base chat or audio. Many companies have found that a single support representative can work with several customers simultaneously when using a text-based service. The benefits of voice/audio are obvious but add significantly to the cost.

E-Learning as a Service

An even more sophisticated way to deliver product and service support is by using one of the many video-based, e-learning services. These are offered in two ways: first as an archived or library product; and second, as real time. A real-time service that represents one of the new breeds of offerings is Essential Talk from the Essential Talk Network. This service operates like a radio talk show with broadcast quality sound and interactivity using either posted chat or phone-in. One way to use this service is to record a session on a particular topic and then make it available from a library as users require the information. These sessions could be comprehensive "how to's" with voice, slides, documents, and diagrams made available to the user.

Help Desks and Call Centres

A help desk or call centre is a place where all customer contact is directed. Staff of the call centre has access to the necessary information to provide service to customers. There are a number of organisations that provide this service for a variety of companies thereby keeping the costs down for each organisation.

Delivery Status

If you deliver a product through one of the logistics companies, you can use their information service to help keep customers informed of the delivery status. Each of these organisations will provide a link for you to pass on the customers, so they can check status. For instance, if you sell books or office supplies you can have them shipped to the customer by one of these companies. By letting the customer know the waybill by e-mail or at a secure place on the site, the customer can track the order from the time it leaves your premises. There are two benefits to this service. Customers have up-to-date information available any time of the day or night, and they do not have to call into your organisation to get it; this way do not have to add staff for this purpose.

Value of Customer Knowledge

Customer knowledge is one of the most valuable assets your organisation has. Gathering demographic and geographic information about your customers allows you to segment them for special attention. You may want to inform customers of a particular product that is of interest to single males aged 25-35. Having a database containing this information will allow you to send an e-flyer to tell them about the product.When you remember that twenty per cent of your customers gives you eighty per cent of your revenue, it is important to know who that twenty per cent is.

Delivering to Customers

There is no better way to ensure customer satisfaction than to deliver to their expectations. Make sure you have the logistics right-packaging, shipping, delivery to the customer's door, and handling returns.

Privacy and Security

If you gather information about customers at your online business, you will need to create a privacy statement. You are also required to give customers the opportunity to"opt in" or "opt out" of providing information. There are a number of services on the web that help to build a comprehensive privacy statement. By simply entering your contact data and how you will use the information you will collect, the service creates a statement to include in your site.

5

BUILDING CUSTOMER LOYALTY

Customer loyalty describes the tendency of a customer to choose one business or product over another for a particular need. In the packaged goods industry, customers may be described as being "brand loyal" because they tend to choose a certain brand of soap more often than others. Note the use of the word "choose" though; customer loyalty becomes evident when choices are made and actions taken by customers. Customers may express high satisfaction levels with a company in a survey, but satisfaction does not equal loyalty. Loyalty is demonstrated by the actions of the customer; customers can be very satisfied and still not be loyal.

Customer loyalty has become a catch-all term for the end result of many marketing approaches where customer data is used. You can say relationship marketing or database marketing or permission marketing or CRM, and what you are really talking about is trying to increase customer loyalty—getting customers to choose to buy or visit more. Increased customer loyalty is the end result, the desired benefit of these programmes. All of the above approaches have two elements in common—they increase both customer retention and the Lifetime value of customers.

Customer loyalty is the result of well-managed customer retention programmes; customers who are targeted by a retention programme demonstrate higher loyalty to a business. All customer retention programmes rely on communicating with customers, giving them encouragement to remain active and choosing to do business with a company.

You want customers to do something, to take action. You want them to visit your website, make a purchase, sign up for a newsletter. And once they do it for the first time, you want them to continue doing business with you, especially since you probably paid big money to get them to do business with you the first time. You don't want to pay big money the second time. You want to create a "loyal" customer who engages in profitable behaviour.

PLANNING FOR CUSTOMER LOYALTY

If you currently retain 70 per cent of your customers and you start a programme to improve that to 80 per cent, you'll add an additional 10 per cent to your growth rate. Particularly because of the high cost of landing new customers versus the high profitability of a loyal customer base, you might want to reflect upon your current business strategy.

These four factors will greatly affect your ability to build a loyal customer base:

1. Products that are highly differentiated from those of the competition.
2. Higher-end products where price is not the primary buying factor.
3. Products with a high service component.
4. Multiple products for the same customer.

Market to Your Own Customers

Giving a lot of thought to your marketing programmes aimed at current customers is one aspect of building customer loyalty. When you buy a new car, many dealers will within minutes try to sell you an extended warranty, an alarm system, and maybe rustproofing. It's often a very easy sale and costs the dealer almost nothing to make.

Use Complaints to Build Business

When customers aren't happy with your business they usually won't complain to you—instead, they'll probably complain to just about everyone else they know—and take their business to your competition next time. That's why an increasing number of businesses are making follow-up calls or mailing satisfaction questionnaires after the sale is made. They find that if they promptly follow up and resolve a customer's complaint, the customer might be even more likely to do business than the average customer who didn't have a complaint.

In many business situations, the customer will have many more interactions after the sale with technical, service, or customer support people than they did with the sales people. So if you're serious about retaining customers or getting referrals, these interactions are the ones that are really going to matter. They really should be handled with the same attention and focus that sales calls get because in a way they are sales calls for repeat business.

Reach Out To Your Customers

Contact with current customers is a good way to build their loyalty. The more the customer sees someone from your firm, the more likely you'll get the next order. Send Christmas cards, see them at trade shows, stop by to make sure everything's okay.

Send a simple newsletter to your customers-tell them about the great things that are happening at your firm and include some useful information for them. Send them copies of any media clippings about your firm. Invite them to free seminars. The more they know about you, the more they see you as someone out to help them, the more they know about your accomplishments-the more loyal a customer they will be.

Loyal Customers and Loyal Workforces

Building customer loyalty will be a lot easier if you have a loyal workforce—not at all a given these days. It is especially important for you to retain those employees who interact with customers such as sales people, technical support, and customer-service people. Many companies give a lot of attention to retaining sales people but little to support people.

The increasing trend today is to send customer-service and technical-support calls into queue for the next available person. This builds no personal loyalty and probably less loyalty for the firm. Before you go this route, be sure this is what your customers prefer. Otherwise I'd assign a specific support person to every significant customer.

LOYALTY RETAILING

Treating your customer as a guest isn't a bad idea, it's just short sighted. A guest may be pleased and satisfied with a particular visit, but it doesn't translate into the same affinity and desire to return again and again, that is felt when visiting a good friend.

Friendships are special things. You go out of your way to see friends. You care about their health, what they need, and you enjoy their company. Guests are frequently unwelcome and sometimes they know it. Friends are rarely unwelcome. It takes two to create a friendship. Retailers have to get to know their customers and listen to their concerns in order to establish the trust necessary for a strong, loyal, long-lived friendship.

It is no wonder that loyalty, guest, and personalised programmes are becoming big business. They all share the same basic goal of capturing market share and gaining repeat business. Smart retailers should be looking at these programmes as a way to turn their customers into friends. It takes patience. It takes more than one visit. However, as friendships develop, great things start to happen. The increased loyalty brings referrals (new friendships). It makes marketing efforts more efficient and effective. It can help a retailer gain co-op advertising from vendors designed to meet their friends' needs. Friends visit more and spend more because they know that this retailer is a friend who cares about they want.

Friendship is the most effective branding a store can ever use. It isn't loyalty programmes that set retailers apart from their competition, it is friendships. In this series, we'll explore the pros, the cons, the alternatives, and the best practices of loyalty programmes and frequent shopper cards. Best of all, we'll use these ideas to show how retailers can build friendships with their customers.

PROTECTING CUSTOMER PRIVACY

It's no secret that retailers want to increase their sales, and creating loyalty is an excellent way to do it. How are retailers going about creating loyalty and is it working?

Are loyalty programmes helping retailers establish friendships with their customers or are they backfiring?

Grocery retailers have been collecting extensive data on their shoppers habits through their frequent shopper programmes for more than a decade. Many non-grocery retailers have their own version of frequent shopper programmes. These programmes come in several different varieties, from the simple to the complex.

Frequent shopper programmes do give retailers the ability to get to know the buying habits of the users of the cards or online profiles. However, if the data is handled incorrectly, it can destroy the trust necessary for a strong, loyal, long-lived friendship. Why? Because consumers are becoming more privacy and security savvy. They are increasingly reluctant to share personal information. Most will only share once they see a clear benefit, and then many still only share reluctantly.

In order to forge strong friendships with customers, retailers are going to have to create stronger privacy policies and make them binding even through mergers and acquisitions. Consumers need to know that their purchasing data isn't going to result in unwelcome postal or e-mail solicitations, tele-marketing calls, or stolen identities. The retailers that can show a strong respect for their customers' privacy are the ones that will win.

Retailers offer frequent shopper cards to their customers so that they can better understand them. Understanding their customers allows retailers to make better assortment decisions and improve the efficiency of the supply chain. A more efficient supply chain and better assortment allow retailers to target their customers with goods and services that meet the customers' needs. Meeting needs creates loyal customers and drives retail sales.

When the data is used strictly to aid in category management, it can be a tremendous asset. If the retailer shows a lack of respect for customer privacy or customer intelligence, it won't inspire loyalty and may become an annoyance. How many frequent shopper cards do you have in your wallet right now? Chances are if you live in an area with more than one supermarket, you have several.

The consumers are not showing loyalty to the store by signing up for their cards. They are showing that they will do what they have to in order to get the discounts. They are submitting to being tracked and are willing to present their cards in order to keep their food bills within budget.

Anticipating needs is the holy grail of loyalty marketing. When retailers can anticipate their customers' needs they begin to win loyalty. Retailers who match products to their customers' behaviour are focused on their shoppers. Using collected data to target their product categories and give customers what they need, when they need it is what these programmes are supposed to be about. The best category management has always focused on the customer, even before the advent of loyalty programmes.

Smart retailers combine their targeting with their category management and learn how to use their data in collaboration with manufacturers. Both retailers and manufacturers bring unique knowledge and insights to the table. Combining business knowledge of both with a customer purchase history database makes it much easier to target specific offers to specific customers.

VALUE OF PERSONALISATION

Recognising a customer when they walk through the

door or sign-on to a website allows the retailer to tailor the shopping experience for each customer. By recognising each shopper as an unique individual with their own tastes, needs and desires, retailers can establish friendships and create customer loyalty. The information to personalise can come from different sources. When customers become members or order from Web sites, or when they sign-up for frequent shopper cards, information is collected. It frequently includes name and address. Sometimes salary history, social security, driver's license, marital and family data is collected. Then, as the customers make purchases, their purchase history is added to the database.

Even websites that may not directly ask for personal data, might track the "clickstream"—clicks, time spent per page, items selected, but abandoned, and similar information—all in order to find out more about their customers and their behaviour. The clickstream data becomes a useful resource for data mining tools that predict gender, age, income, preferences, and a customer's willingness to purchase.

Are retailers walking a fine line between providing a valuable service and invading customers' privacy when they use their data? Of course retailers want an edge in knowing what product to pitch while you're at their site or in their store. Of course they want to learn the elasticity in the price of an item. If it allows retailers deliver to you the right offer at the right time, is it worth it? Many customers believe so. There is great value in having drug interactions recognised and corrected in the pharmacy instead of after an incident. There is value in being informed of a sale on your favourite items so that you can stock up.

Personalised service best comes from retailers listening to their customers, learning their needs, finding out what they like and how they like it. Every retailer can personalise some portion of their customer interaction. The best part of it for retailers is that it doesn't have to take buckets of money to get started. Just remember your best customers' names.

VALUE OF INTERACTION

Friendship is the most effective branding a store can ever use. It isn't loyalty programmes that set retailers apart from their competition, it is friendships. Friendships are forged from human interaction. Getting rid of the cold and impersonal, and adding the personal touch is the way to recognise every shopper as an unique individual. By valuing their customers' feelings, tastes, needs and desires, retailers create friendships and build customer loyalty.

Many retailers, large and small, brick-and-mortar and pure-play, have found ways to build friendships. From letting a customer try a product in the store before they buy it, to soliciting feedback on products and giving customers a way to share their experiences with other customers, retailers are treating customers like friends, not just guests.

Retailers find that as friendships develop, great things start to happen. The increased loyalty brings referrals and new friends into the store. Customers start stopping by more often just to see what's going on and what's new. Both retailers and customers benefit from the interaction. In the next instalment we'll start the wrap up of the retail loyalty series with an exploration of how respect plays a large part in creating loyalty.

VALUE OF RESPECT

Are we fast approaching a world of retailing where every

consumer is just a walking profile that retailers will be able to target with precision? How can a retailer use its customers' data in a way that respects their privacy and their individuality?

In redefining the way consumers shop in the future, retailers need to walk the fine line between respecting their customers' time by presenting a targeted selection and invading their customers' privacy. Retailers who are able to use their loyalty and customer relationship programmes wisely will become the big winners.

In order for a retailer to become a loyal friend they first need to become a brand, and then infuse their brand with human qualities. Humanised retailers create an atmosphere where customers are able to relate with it and form emotional attachments, much like the way they relate to human beings.

This type of branding is not the same as the creative process used by marketers. It is the core essence of a retailer—who they are and what they represent to consumers. Retailers who humanise their brands react to their customers in a manner that shows their own humanity. These retailers respect the customers and communities they serve because it is a sound business decision and the right thing to do. They seek to belong to the community because the community is made up of their customers and potential customers. As part of the community, retailers gain respect as "one of us," who live and breathe in our neighbourhoods.

Communities can be geographic or demographic, virtual or three-dimensional. As long as it is a space where interaction takes place, there is the potential for community. In building their stores or Web sites to reach their community, retailers can begin the branding and loyalty process.

As members of the community, retailers gain entry into their customers' lives. This allows the retailer to begin the courtship of friendship and personalisation. By showing respect, interacting, providing help and information, and respecting customers' privacy, the retailer becomes a friend.

Once a friend, customers are willing to open up and share their private information. Information that the customers give to help their friends get to know and help them, and in return, the customers help the retailers with their loyalty. After all, everyone is more loyal to those they have shared their secrets and private information with, and have proven themselves worthy of the honour.

Using a customer's private information to show her exciting and interesting solutions and meeting her unique needs wins friendship. It is about personalising, not targeting. It reinforces the retailer's brand and the friendship with the customer. It creates a win-win for both retailer and consumer.

In being seen as a unique and special person inside a larger community that both the customer and the retailer belong to, the targeting process is humanised. It becomes desirable personalisation instead of an annoying commercial targeting tactic. Personalising a friend's shopping experience enforces branding.

Retailers need to remember that their brand is their personality, what makes them unique and personal. Retailers who shift the focus of their marketing away from their brand and onto consumer targeting may face the loss of their community appeal and find out that they no longer belong.

Customer Loyalty Programmes

Customer loyalty is key to business growth. After all,

keeping an existing customer costs far less than acquiring a new one. Finding new customers is important, but unless you are able to retain those customers it's unlikely that you'll be able to achieve the bottom line you need for significant growth in your business.

Customer loyalty programmes can go a long way toward helping you improve customer retention because they provide a low-cost incentive for existing customers to continue buying your products and services. Customer loyalty programmes come in a wide variety of shapes and forms. It's up to you to decide which one is right for your business. With that in mind, here are some of your options:

Prepaid Discounts

Prepaid discounts offer customers a reason to buy a certain amount of product or services in advance. For example, a bagel shop could run a baker's dozen discount, offering customers a punch card good for thirteen bagels. The cost of the punch card would be equivalent to the normal price of a dozen bagels, thus rewarding the customer with a free bagel for buying twelve in advance.

Buying Level Discounts

Buying level discounts are very similar to prepaid discounts with one difference—instead of being rewarded for buying products or services in advance, the customer is rewarded once they reach a certain level of purchasing. Going back to our bagel shop example, the customer would still use a punch card. But instead of paying for a dozen bagels in advance, the bagels would be purchased as needed and the free bagel reward given after the punch card has been "filled"—indicating that the customer has reached the twelve bagel threshold.

The disadvantage of buying level discounts is that they have become so commonplace that many people won't participate in them simply to avoid cluttering up their wallet or purse. The key is to make the reward enticing enough that they can't refuse.

Membership Programmes

Some retailers have been very successful at using membership programmes to attract and retain customers over a long period of time. Membership-based retail operations leverage their buying power to offer discounted prices—but only after the customer has demonstrated his loyalty by becoming a member. Admittedly, membership-based retail is not right for every business. But you might want to consider offering a membership discount option as a way to reward committed customers.

Upgrades

Upgrades are another cost-effective way to reward customer loyalty. In most cases, the costs of upgrades are negligible compared to the feelings of goodwill they create in your customers. Airlines have been using upgrades for years, offering passengers a bump up to first- and business-class as rewards in their frequent flyer programmes. These upgrades don't cost the airline anything since the number of people paying full fare for the better seats is rarely enough to fill them. However, by using upgrades as a reward, the airlines are able to keep their customers coming back time and time again.

EARNING CUSTOMER LOYALTY

Customer loyalty is the practice of finding, attracting, and retaining your customers who regularly purchase from you. Customer loyalty is not customer satisfaction. Customer satisfaction is the basic entry point of good business practices. Your small business should provide satisfaction to all your customers.

Loyalty cards and programmes have their rewards and pitfalls. Rewarding customers for spending more rupees can create a vicious cycle of creating customers who want rewards and will look anywhere to obtain them.

Software, card programmes, and loyalty schemes are the tools of customer loyalty programmes but they aren't the essence of loyalty. To build loyalty, you must earn it. Look at the following ways to earn more customer loyalty for your small business:

1. *Company loyalty first*: Customer loyalty is a 2-way street. How can you expect customer loyalty if you don't practice company loyalty? Are you loyal to your best customers or are you giving discounts and extra attention to new customers? Loyalty is about being fanatical with devotion to your best customers.
2. *Employee loyalty second*: Any customer loyalty programme must factor in the front line of the business. It's the point of contact between customer and employee that sets the foundation of repeat business.
3. *Quench the thirst*: Consumers are thirsty for trust following corporate scandals and the general distrust of corporations. If your small business is not trustworthy, your odds of establishing customer loyalty are diminished.

4. *Finding loyalty:* Any small business wishing to start a customer loyalty initiative needs first to identify important customers and understand their customer's behaviours. Use whatever tools, software, and data-mining techniques to locate your repeat, regular customers. Equally vital is to know your profit margins. Don't offer discounts until you know the impact on your bottom line.
5. *Reward customer retention*: The key metric to track in your customer loyalty programme is customer retention. How many customers are defecting? How many clients are retained? Measuring customer retention is half the battle. Your staff must be rewarded for retention. Your small business doesn't have to be like big corporations who talk retention but reward sales people for bringing in new customers only.
7. *Use customer-centric language*: It's easy to think you put the customer first. However, take a closer look at your marketing communications. How many times does your literature refer to "we" the company versus "you" the customer? Go back and speak from the customer's perspective.
8. *Bolster customer communications*: Part of customer loyalty and retention are maintaining regular contact with your most profitable customers. Communication to your best customers should take the form of showing your appreciation and providing new learning experiences to add value to your customer's life. Send special thankyou notes, surprise gifts, and regular communications such as newsletters to connect with them.
9. *Use the Small Business Advantage*: Small business will always have the advantage in connecting with customers and building a solid relationship. Your

passion for helping customers with your products and services is difficult for large companies to replicate.

Win the customer service game by putting customer loyalty to work in your small business. It is more than cards and software.

6

CUSTOMER-CENTRED COMMUNICATION

One of the main goals of any business is to achieve reoccurring sales and referrals. To achieve this goal, the business owner needs to ensure the customer is happy with the service or product being offered. A customer's happiness can be from effective communication on the part of the business owners and associates.

Customer-centred communications means ensuring that every employee in your organisation has an intimate knowledge of your customers' wants, needs and expectations through the distribution of information. In order to foster real, fundamental change in the way we use information to create value for the customer, we must first understand the challenges that lie ahead for creating this change:

1. How do we begin to emphasise what we communicate to our employees, after so many years of focusing on how we communicate?
2. How do we use information to help our employees get closer to our customers, when our corporate culture may lack basic trust in people?
3. How do we harness employee talents, insights and energies toward serving enduser customers, when

we've encouraged them to spend so much time focusing on serving each other?

4. How do we use information as a strategic tool to make it easier to manage our organisations?
5. How do we treat employees as partners in our business, and set the expectation that they behave the same way?

The old model of employee communication was linear and inward looking. It was linear in that information about customers typically entered the organisation through one or two sources. Information was watered down and passed on until when it reached the support functions it was nothing more than "nice to know" information. The old model was inward-looking because it relied heavily on the internal customer concept. One department only need know enough to serve its internal customers and had no regard for what was happening outside the organisation.

The customer-centred communications model is fundamentally different. It's chaotic. As we've learned in recent years, order is born out of chaos. It's outward looking. It relies heavily on an employee's "right to know" customer information real customer information direct form the customer's own words, in order to make effective decisions, solve problems more quickly, and develop objectives which focus on serving the end-user customer.

COMMUNICATING EFFECTIVELY

Communicating successfully with customers is an essential part of doing business, and many businesses work hard to have good communication with their customers. But, when dealing with customers who are blind or have low vision, customers who are deaf or hard of hearing, or customers who have disabilities that impair speech, many business owners and employees are uncomfortable or are not sure what to do. This lesson provides the answers.

Businesses are expected to communicate effectively with customers who have vision, hearing, or speech disabilities, and are responsible for taking the steps that are needed for effective communication. Business owners or managers must decide what assistance is appropriate, depending on the nature of the communication and the customer's normal method of communication.

The rules are intentionally flexible. Different businesses may need different solutions, because the nature of their communications are different. Also, different customers need different solutions, because the nature of their disabilities are different.

Practical Solutions to Communication Problems

The aim is to figure out practical solutions that allow you to communicate with customers who have disabilities and fit with your type of business. Some easy solutions work in relatively simple and straightforward situations. Other, more extensive solutions are needed where the information being communicated is more extensive or complex.

1. For relatively simple and straightforward transactions:

   (*a*) You can speak or read information to a customer who is blind or has low vision.

   (*b*) You can use facial or body gestures that express information, point to information, or write notes to communicate with a customer who is deaf or hard of hearing.

(*c*) You can read notes written by a customer who has a speech disability, or read or listen to the words communicated by the customer's "communication board."

(*d*) Customers who are blind may also need assistance in finding an item or in manuevering through your business's space.

2. For more extensive or complex communications:

(*a*) For people who are blind or have low vision, printed information can be provided in large print, in Braille, on a computer disk, or in an audio format, depending on what is usable for the particular customer. A magnifying glass can also help a person with low vision to read printed materials.

(*b*) For people who are deaf or hard of hearing, spoken information can be provided using a sign language interpreter, an oral interpreter, a printed transcript of the words that are usually spoken, or a service called "real-time captioning" which is explained later.

Usually the customer will tell you what technique he or she needs or will ask which ones you provide. Or, you can ask what technique he or she normally uses to understand printed information (if he or she has a vision disability) or spoken information (if he or she has a hearing disability). This information is helpful in deciding how to provide effective communication.

UNDERSTANDING YOUR COMMUNICATION STYLES

Understanding your personal style of communicating will go a long way toward helping you to create good and lasting impressions on others. By becoming more aware of how others perceive you, you can adapt more readily to their styles of communicating. This does not mean you have to be a chameleon, changing with every personality you meet. Instead, you can make another person more comfortable with you by selecting and emphasising certain behaviours that fit within your personality and resonate with another.

Every time we speak, we choose and use one of four basic communication styles: assertive, aggressive, passive and passive-aggressive.

1. Assertive.
2. Aggressive.
3. Passive.
4. Passive-aggressive

Assertive Communication

The most effective and healthiest form of communication is the assertive style. It's how we naturally express ourselves when our self-esteem is intact, giving us the confidence to communicate without games and manipulation.

When we are being assertive, we work hard to create mutually satisfying solutions. We communicate our needs clearly and forthrightly. We care about the relationship and strive for a win/win situation. We know our limits and refuse to be pushed beyond them just because someone else wants or needs something from us. Surprisingly, assertive is the style most people use least.

Aggressive Communication

Aggressive communication always involves manipulation. We may attempt to make people do what we want by inducing guilt (hurt) or by using intimidation and control tactics (anger). Covert or overt, we simply want our needs met—and right now! Although there are a few arenas where aggressive behaviour is called for (i.e., sports or war), it will never work in a relationship. Ironically, the more aggressive sports rely heavily on team members and rational coaching strategies. Even war might be avoided if we could learn to be more assertive and negotiate to solve our problems.

Passive Communication

Passive communication is based on compliance and hopes to avoid confrontation at all costs. In this mode we don't talk much, question even less, and actually do very little. We just don't want to rock the boat. Passives have learned that it is safer not to react and better to disappear than to stand up and be noticed.

Passive-aggressive Communication

A combination of styles, passive-aggressive avoids direct confrontation (passive), but attempts to get even through manipulation (aggressive). If you've ever thought about making that certain someone who needs to be "taught a thing or two" suffer (even just a teeny bit), you've stepped pretty close to (if not on into) the devious and sneaky world of the passive-aggressive. This style of communication often leads to office politics and rumour-mongering.

Clearly, for many reasons, the only healthy communication style is assertive communication. Surely you can identify many people in your own life that favour each of the four styles. Most of us use a combination of these four styles, depending on the person or situation. The styles we choose generally depend on what our past experiences have taught us will work best to get our needs met in each specific situation.

If you take a really good look at yourself, you've probably used each throughout your lifetime.

Understanding the four basic types of communication will help you learn how to react most effectively when confronted with a difficult person. It will also help you recognize when you are using manipulative behaviour to get your own needs met. Remember, you always have a choice as to which communication style you use. If you're serious about taking control of your life, practice being more assertive. It will help you diffuse anger, reduce guilt and build relationships—both personally and professionally.

IMPROVING YOUR COMMUNICATION SKILLS

Learning better communication skills requires a lot of effort because cooperation between people is a much more complex and mentally demanding process than coercing, threatening or just grabbing what you want. The needs of two people are involved rather than just the needs of one. And thinking about the wants of two people is a giant step beyond simply feeling one's own wants. The journey from fighting over the rubber ducky to learning how to share it is the longest journey a child will ever make, a journey that leads far beyond childhood. Reaching this higher level of skill and fulfilment in living and working with others requires effort, conscious attention, and practice with other people.

A second reason that learning more effective and satisfying communication skills does not happen automatically is that our way of communicating with others is deeply woven into our personalities, into the history of our hearts.

A third side of the communications mountain concerns self-observation. In the course of living our attention is generally pointed out toward other people and the world around us. As we talk and joke, comfort others and negotiate with them, we are often lost in the flow of interaction. Communicating more cooperatively involves exerting a gentle influence to guide conversations toward happier endings for all the participants. But in order to guide or steer an unfolding process, a person needs to be able to observe that process. So communicating more cooperatively and more satisfyingly requires that we learn how to participate in our conversations and observe them at the very same time! It takes a while to grow into this participating and observing at the same time. At first we look back on conversations that we have had and try to understand what went well and what went badly. Gradually we can learn to bring that observing awareness into our conversations.

A final reason that learning new communication skills takes effort is that we are surrounded by a flood of bad examples. Every day movies and TV offer us a continuing stream of vivid images of sarcasm, fighting, cruelty, fear and mayhem. And as beer and cigarette advertisers have proven beyond a shadow of a doubt, you can get millions of people to do something if you just show enough vivid pictures of folks already doing it. So at some very deep level we are being educated by the mass media to fail in our relationships. For every movie about people making peace with one another, there seem to be a hundred movies about people hacking each other to death with chainsaws or literally kicking one another in the face, which are not actions that will help you or me solve problems at home or at the office. Learning to relate to others generally involves following examples, but our examples of interpersonal skill and compassion are few and far between.

You will look at improving your communication skills as a long journey, like crossing a mountain range, so that you will feel more like putting effort and attention into the process, and thus will get more out of it. Living a fully human life is surprisingly similar to playing baseball or playing the violin. Getting better at each requires continual practice.

Get more done, have more fun, which could also be stated as better coordination of your life activities with the life activities of the people who are important to you. Living and working with others are communication-intensive activities. The better we understand what other people are feeling and wanting, and the more clearly others understand our goals and feelings, the easier it will be to make sure that everyone is pulling in the same direction.

Since there is a lot of mutual imitation in everyday communication, when we adopt a more compassionate and respectful attitude toward our conversation partners, we invite and influence them to do the same toward us. When we practice the combination of responsible honesty and attentiveness recommended here, we are more likely to engage other people and reach agreements that everyone can live with, we are more likely to get what we want, and for reasons we won't regret later.

Because each person has different talents, there is much to be gained by people working together, and accomplishing together what none could do alone. But because each person also has different needs and views, there will always be some conflict in living and working with others. By understanding more of what goes on in conversations, we can become better team problem solvers and conflict navigators. Learning to listen to others more deeply can increase our confidence that we will be able to engage in a dialogue of genuine give and take, and be able to help generate problem solutions that meet more of everyone's needs.

Because every action we take toward others reverberates for months (or years) inside our own minds and bodies, adopting a more peaceful and creative attitude in our interaction with others can be a significant way of lowering our own stress levels. Even in unpleasant situations, we can feel good about our own skilful responses.

Learning to communicate better will get us involved with exploring two big questions: "What's going on inside of me?" and "What's going on inside of you?" Modern life is so full of distractions and entertainments that many people don't know their own hearts very well, nor the hearts of others nearby. Exercises in listening can help us listen more carefully and reassure our conversation partners that we really do understand what they are going through. Exercises in self-expression can help us ask for what we want more clearly and calmly.

CHALLENGES OF EFFECTIVE COMMUNICATION

A brief summary of some challenges to effective communication are described below.

Careful Listening

Listen first and acknowledge what you hear, even if you don't agree with it, before expressing your experience or point of view. In order to get more of your conversation partner's attention in tense situations, pay attention first: listen and give a brief restatement of what you have heard before you express your own needs or position. The kind of listening recommended here separates acknowledging from approving or agreeing. Acknowledging another person's thoughts and feelings does not have to mean that you approve of or agree with that person's actions or way of experiencing, or that you will do whatever someone asks. Some of the deeper levels of this first step include learning to listen to your own heart, and learning to encounter identities and integrities quite different from your own, while still remaining centred in your own sense of self.

Explain Your Conversational Intent

You can help your conversation partners cooperate with you and reduce possible misunderstandings by starting important conversations with a stated invitation to join you in the specific kind of conversation you want to have. The more the conversation is going to mean to you, the more important it is for your conversation partner to understand the big picture. Most conversations express one or another of about thirty basic intentions, which imply different kinds of cooperation from your conversation partners. They can play their role in specific conversations much better if you clarify for yourself, and then identify for them, the role you are asking for, rather than leaving them to guess what you might be wanting.

Express Yourself

Slow down and give your listeners more information about what you are experiencing by using a wide range of "I-statements." One way to help get more of your listener's empathy is to express more of the five basic dimensions of your experience. Anytime one person sincerely listens to another, a very creative process is going on in which the listener mentally reconstructs the speaker's experience. The more facets or dimensions of your experience you share with easy-to-grasp "I statements," the easier it will be for your conversation partner to reconstruct your experience accurately and understand what you are feeling. This is equally worthwhile whether you are trying to solve a problem with someone or trying to express appreciation for them.

Expressing yourself this carefully might appear to take longer than your usual quick style of communication. But if you include all the time it takes to unscramble everyday misunderstandings, and to work through the feelings that usually accompany not being understood, expressing yourself more completely can actually take a lot less time. Some deeper levels of this third step include developing the courage to tell the truth, growing beyond blame in understanding painful experiences, and learning to make friends with feelings, your own and other people's, too.

Translate Your Complaints into Requests

In order to get more cooperation from others, whenever possible ask for what you want by using specific, action-oriented, positive language rather than by using generalisations, "why's," "don'ts" or "somebody should's." Help your listeners comply by explaining your requests with a "so that...", "it would help me to... if you would..." or "in order to...." Also, when you are receiving criticism and complaints from others, translate and restate the complaints as action requests.....". Some of the deeper levels of this fourth step include developing a strong enough sense of self-esteem that you can accept being turned down, and learning how to imagine creative solutions to problems, solutions in which everyone gets at least some of their needs met.

Ask Questions Open-endedly

In order to coordinate our life and work with the lives and work of other people, we all need to know more of what other people are feeling and thinking, wanting and planning. But our usual "yes/no" questions actually tend to shut people up rather than opening them up. In order to encourage your conversation partners to share more of their thoughts and feelings, ask "open-ended" rather than "yes/no" questions. Open-ended questions allow for a wide range of responses. For example, asking "How did you like that food/movie /speech/doctor/etc.?" will evoke a more detailed response than "Did you like it?". We explore asking a wide range of open-ended questions. When we ask questions we are using a powerful language tool to focus conversational attention and guide our interaction with others. But many of the questions we have learned to ask are totally fruitless and self-defeating. In general it will be more fruitful to ask "how" questions about the future rather than "why" questions about the past, but there are many more creative possibilities as well. Of the billions of questions we might ask, not all are equally fruitful or illuminating; not all are equally helpful in solving problems together. We explore asking powerfully creative questions from many areas of life. Deeper levels of this fifth step include developing the courage to hear the answers to our questions, to face the truth of what other people are feeling. Also, learning to be comfortable with the process of looking at a situation from different perspectives, and learning to accept that people often have needs, views and tastes different from your own.

Express Appreciations

To build more satisfying relationships with the people around you, express more appreciation, delight, affirmation, encouragement and gratitude. Because life continually requires us to attend to problems and breakdowns, it gets very easy to see in life only what is broken and needs fixing. But satisfying relationships require us to notice and respond to what is delightful, excellent, enjoyable, to work well done, to food well cooked, etc. It is appreciation that makes a relationship strong enough to accommodate differences and disagreements. Thinkers and researchers in several different fields have reached similar conclusions about this: healthy relationships need a core of mutual appreciation. One deeper level of this sixth step is in how you might shift your overall level of appreciation and gratitude, toward other people, toward nature, and toward life and/or a "Higher Power."

Make Good Communication a Part of Life

In order to have your new communication skills available in a wide variety of situations, you will need to practice them in as wide a variety of situations as possible, until, like driving or bicycling, they become "second nature." Another challenge is to practice your evolving communication skills in everyday life, solving problems together, giving emotional support to the important people in your life, and enjoying how you are becoming a positive influence in your world. This challenge includes learning to see each conversation as an opportunity to grow in skill and awareness, each encounter as an opportunity to express more appreciation, each argument as an opportunity to translate your complaints into requests, and so on.

IMPROVE CUSTOMER-CENTRED COMMUNICATION

Some helpful tips to improve customer-centred communication are listed below:

— *Once you have the good, hard answers to the above questions, it's time to take action.* Throw out every theory you know about communicating with employees. Now is the time for fundamental change.

— *It's time to go back to all those technological advances in communications that we've spent so much time and money on improving in our organisations.* Use them! Not to communicate the same information that has been clogging our organisational veins for decades, but to communicate raw, unfiltered customer information which will help your employees create value for your end-user customers.

— *Involve employees in the communications process and hold them accountable.* Find ways to use the communications tools available in your company, along with the talent and enthusiasm of your people, to allow free flow of customer information. Ask them what information they need and want, what will help them contribute more, and how best to deliver it to them. Then, be sure to hold them accountable for knowing the information. Far too many organisations allow their employees to depend on the organisation for feeding them information, instead of providing opportunities to get informed, then holding them accountable for seeking out the information.

— *Examine policies/procedures that may inhibit the flow of communication.* Review your policies and procedures manual or any written guidelines used by management with a fine tooth comb. Do your policies "punish" people for communicating or for seeking out information? For example, a policy which prohibits certain employees from taking action to serve the customer, may be causing your organisation to drift further and further away from a customer-centred environment.

— *Agree on what customer information is important to your organisation.* Consensus should come not only from management, but from employees from throughout your organisation, and most importantly from your customers. Ask your employees what they need and want to know about your customers. Ask your customers want they need and want your employees to know about them.

— *Hit replay before you speak.* Be sure to have a clear picture of the message and then form an outline in your mind before the words are spoken. Know exactly how you want to convey that message to your customer or business associate.

— *Ensure active participation.* A good in person conversation entails eye contact which deems it necessary to be looking at each other during communication. When you and your customer are not looking at each other, it doesn't allow for "active listening". Wait until there is an open, clear line of communication before you speak. By speaking while in another room or with your back turned, it may appear the customer may feel unimportant, which can lead to frustration between you and your customer.

— *Patience really is a virtue.* Don't let your impatience get the best of you when trying to communicate. The true meaning of your message may get misunderstood if you decide you need to tell your customer something too quickly. This could lead to a misperception of your message and then you will need to spend more time trying to explain what the message was you were trying to convey.

— *Remember to listen.* Listen to the customer and answer questions fully. By listening, it displays your commitment to the customer's needs and wants. As a business owner, listening should be done first and then speaking with the customer.

— *Know your audience.* Successful communicators understand their audience because they connect with an aspect of our lives, whether it is personal or professional. When you are in tune with your customer's lives, the business relationship develops on a more personable level. This can be a factor when deciding to go with a company for business.

— *Get the facts.* Effective communicating is driven by having the facts to go along with your message. No small detail is insignificant. For example, when writing down a phone message, be sure to ask for all the correct contact information, the caller's first and last name, and their message.

— *Ask questions.* Ask your customer if they have any questions about your message, whether it be a phone call or presentation. If they do, be sure to answer them honestly.

— *Watch your tone.* The use of the tone in your voice when communicating can mean the difference between getting the correct message across and creating an argument. Be uplifting and encouraging with your tone.

— *Beware of interrupting.* Be careful about interrupting others, particularly your customers. They'll be especially upset if, while they're explaining a problem, you interrupt them and start offering a solution. If you feel you have to interrupt, at least cut to the chase and tell the other person what you think his or her main idea was. That way, the other person at least can confirm or correct you, and in either case save time.

— *Avoid negative questions.* Suppose you say to a customer, "You don't have Word installed?" and he answers "Yes." What does he mean? Yes, you're right, Word is not installed? Or yes, he does have

Word installed? Asking a negative question creates confusion. It's clearer if you phrase the question positively or ask an open-ended question. If you must use the negative, try a question such as "Am I correct that you don't have Word installed?"

— *Be sensitive to technical knowledge.* Chances are, your customers have less technical knowledge than you do. Be careful, therefore, when explaining things to them. If you use acronyms, be sure you identify what the acronym means. The same acronym can mean different things, even in an IT context. Be careful that you don't make two opposite mistakes: either talking over their head or talking down to them. Keep your eyes on customers when you talk to them and be alert to cues indicating that they don't understand. Ask them whether they understand what you're saying, if necessary.

— *Use analogies to explain technical concepts.* A good way to explain a technical idea is to use an analogy. Though they have limitations, analogies are helpful in explaining an unfamiliar idea in terms of a familiar one. When you enter a bank, you don't just go into the vault and get your money. Instead, you go to a window, where the teller verifies your identity and determines that you have enough money. The teller goes to the vault, brings it back to the window, gives it to you, and then you leave.

— *Use positive instead of negative statements.* Your customers are more interested in your capabilities than in your limitations. In other words, they're interested in what you can do, rather than what you can't do. The way you say things to them influences how they perceive you and your department. You can be seen as a roadblock or you can be seen as a partner.

— *Be careful of misinterpreted words and phrases.* Sometimes we say something with innocent intent, but the other person misinterprets it. We mean to say one thing, but our pronunciation or inflection causes us to convey something else.

— *Technical problems and emotional reactions.* When customers have a technical problem, keep in mind that they'll almost always have an emotional reaction as well. Those emotions can range from simple annoyance to outright panic, depending on the importance of the document and the time element involved. If all you do is solve the technical problem and walk away, chances are the customer will still be upset.

— *Keep the customer informed.* Your customers will become upset if you treat them the same way. Keep them informed of developments involving them, particularly with regard to technical problems and outages. In particular, keep them apprised even if nothing is going on. For example, let them know you've contacted the vendor but still haven't heard anything back. No news is still news.

If a customer leaves you a request via voicemail or e-mail, let the customer know you received it, even if you are still in the process of handling it. Doing so gives the customer one less matter to worry about. When a problem is resolved, let the customer know that, too. Nothing is more frustrating to customers than finding out that they could have been working sooner if they had only known.

Get customers involved in the process. Your customers are just as anxious to be served by your organisation as you are to serve them. Invite them on-site to meet with groups of your employees. And not just those from sales and marketing, but from all functions throughout the company. Ask them to give your employees a "report card" on how well the organisation is doing and areas for improvement. Encourage your support employees to make site visits to your customers' locations. The more they understand the customer's experience, the better able they will be to contribute to creating value for that customer.

Review your performance appraisal process. Do you hold your employees accountable for serving the end-user customer? If not, each employee should be involved in helping to develop goals and objectives which measure the impact they have on creating value for the customer. Much of what we have learned from our experiences in employee communications no longer applies. We are piloting a new and different ship on very different waters. We must experiment with new ways and provide breakthroughs to create lasting changes in today's organisations.

7

CUSTOMER SERVICE ETIQUETTE

Business etiquette isn't only about how well you behave during meetings, luncheons or dinners; it's also about how well you treat your fellow employees and customers. Treat everyone who comes through your door as a valued customer. Try not to typecast or profile them because of their appearance.

You can't take back an insult to a possible customer. Usually you won't even know it has occurred because the customer won't return to your store. Instead, he/she will be more than happy to tell all of their friends about your poor customer service and rude employees. Most businesses should know that this doesn't lose just one dissatisfied customer; by the time that customer has finished recounting their bad experience to friends and family, up to ten potential customers have been lost.

More and more companies are realising that poor customer service will result, not only, in no growth but in a decline from which it will be very difficult to recover. Getting new customers can cost up to five times more than keeping current customers. Training employees in common courtesy and polite behaviour will not only retain the customers you now depend on, but will also bring in new customers who enjoy being treated like people, not like commodities.

PRINCIPLES OF CUSTOMER SERVICE ETIQUETTE

Principles of customer service etiquette should be integrated into every facet of your organisation because providing superior customer service is the most effective way to differentiate your business from the competition.

Many employees will walk onto a job with little or no knowledge of how to interact or communicate with customers and without any appreciation of the importance of delivering exceptional customer service.

Employers have a responsibility to set and effectively communicate the ground rules for how an employee should operate within their company. Often an employee is issued a manual or orientation without any formal training on the company's unique culture or way of conducting business. With this lack of understanding, you have employees in effect defining the company's policies based on their social norms, which leads to the loss of productivity, morale, and profitability.

Empower your employees by teaching them the six principles of customer service etiquette. Properly train and educate your employees on how to interact and communicate with customers to deliver superior customer service, cultivate long-term relationships with clients, build customer loyalty, and differentiate your business from the competition.

The principles of customer service etiquette are:

1. *Smile and demonstrate good manners.* Teach employees to smile, leading by example. Establish a culture of high quality customer service and commit to deliver superior service whether over the phone or face-to-face.

2. Make customers feel comfortable, valued, and appreciated.
3. Treat customers with respect, empathy, and efficiency.
4. Listen actively to be responsive and exceed customer expectations.
5. Effectively resolve the customer's problem.
6. Say "Thank you" and "Please" graciously.

Build prosperous relationships by treating customers as you want to be treated.

Any business, online or storefront, must operate on the basis that customer service is the most critical aspect in business success. Businesses can benefit from using customer service excellence tips which may mean the difference between success and failure. Every small business owner must take the necessary steps to make customer service happen.

A business marketing plan had better take into account that customers are the most important factor - both the acquisition of new customers as well as the retention of existing customers. A successful business marketing strategy puts customer needs and customer satisfaction at the forefront.

Word of mouth is very important, it may not make a business succeed, but a bad reputation can kill one. Remember this as an important service excellence tip, happy customers tell only two or three people about their experience, however unhappy customers will tell an average of ten others! So while it may take a while for your business to grow but it can die very easily.

Happy customers are those who find that all that they needed was provided, and who felt as though they were important to you. The more you personalise the service you give to your customers, the more likely they are to feel as though they have been treated well. One of the tips among customer service excellence tips is avoiding generic responses when confronted with questions and concerns from customers.

Good customer service means being able to talk to a human, whether on the phone or over the internet. An already frustrated customer has little patience for sieving through endless web page FAQs. There is even less tolerance of dealing with a lengthy automated telephone "help" line. You've had this experience; you know how easy it is to turn an angry customer into an ex-customer. Check out your own help line; see if an average customer can navigate your web page FAQs quickly and effectively.

Any comprehensive list of customer service excellence tips must include something about customer complaint resolution. Though there may be several things which are out your hands, such as back orders at your supplier, or post office error, your customers are not interested in excuses. Though they may be willing to accept apologies explaining the situation, they really want to have the situation fixed as quickly as possible.

PLEASING YOUR CUSTOMERS

There are two qualities that separate those who succeed from those who do not. One is the ability to assess self-performance and to identify challenges and areas for improvement. The other skill is to actually make the changes that have been identified.

This may sound easy, but most people do not do it. Why? It is difficult to change habits and styles that have been in place for a long time. After changes have been made, it can be difficult to keep in place. After all, how many people actually retain their New Years resolutions for more than a few weeks?

These skills are essential in the realm of business success. Survival of the fittest dictates that those who can best adapt to the current local environment are the ones who will survive. This is still true for humans, although modern society offers us a comfortable enough lifestyle that we do not have to worry about competing for essentials like food. In the business world, however, survival of the fittest does mean a struggle for the life of your business.

Effective change happens slowly. Gradual change works because it is easier to get started and more likely to last. Effective change also needs to be well planned. Take some time out from your normal routine to sit down and take a long, honest look at the way things are running. Make a thorough business plan and then stick to it!

There are several strategies that you can keep in mind while you make your plan.

1. *First of all, maintain a mutual respect between your business and your customers.* There should be a loving relationship between you and your clientele. After all, they sustain your enterprise. You give them products they need. If you feel anything short of love for your customers, then look at them in a different light. Think of them as the lifeblood of your business, and focus on how essential they are. Your customers should be people you enjoy seeing and doing business with. They should not be an annoyance to you.
2. *Now keep in mind that your customers should be deserving of this love, respect and care that you will offer them.* This will best be accomplished if your business plan includes a way to effectively choose your target audience. You need to figure out who is in need of your product and who has the resources to purchase it. Do not forget to target people who

have a lot in common with you. This is a good start to establishing a healthy, trusting relationship between you and your customers.

3. *Understand your customers.* Focus on what they need. If you can not fulfil their needs they will not stay around. And there is an easy way to find out what they need: ask! They will tell if there is something particular you can help them with. Sometimes, you may need to do a little soul-searching along with them, as they may not even be sure of what their needs are. Ask focused, directed questions to help them figure out exactly what it is they want, then focus on how you can provide this.
4. *A good way to meet your customers needs and establish a respectful relationship is to help them with issues that do not revolve around your store or business.* Fix and help them with products that they purchased somewhere else. Offer recommendations on other non-competing businesses around town. Help them with personal troubles by listening to their frustrations about their families. Often it is not even necessary to provide them with solutions; they might just want somebody to listen to them.

All of this helps you establish a healthy, trusting, and loving relationship with your client base. By listening to their needs and giving them what they want, you will impress them enough that they will return again and again. The end result? You have a successful, profitable business, and a healthy and happy community of customers and friends!

Have you said something positive and nice to everyone you have come into contact today? Do you smile at everyone you past by? If not you should start making it a practice. Learn to treat everyone with respect and kindness in your life and business. Creating that aura of confidence and kindness will elevate how people see you making it more likely that they will consider what services you provide.

What would you think of some person trying to sell you something by using deceit and trickery. What would you do if a salesperson treated you rudely and with disrespect as they were presenting their product? Would you really want to do business with people that treat you so? Probably not and that is why you need to be honest and caring in your dealings with the public if you want to establish a lasting and prosperous venture. Before publishing your advertising review it and make certain that it is not misleading or disrespectful to those you are promoting to.

Be courteous in all your dealings with customers and prospects since they are the life blood of your business. Seek out ways to provide services and goods that are beneficial and desirable to your clients. Make the feel like they are receiving an exceptional value from what you offer. The more happy the potential consumer is the more likely that they will continue to use you instead of searching elsewhere. How the consumer views you will determine many things like purchases and continued use of your services.

You need to setup lines of communication to answer questions and concerns. One of the best ways to do that is to have a help desk setup on your web site. Be sure to provide prompt and courteous answers to your customers and prospects. If there is a problem find a solution to it and resolve the issue in an efficient and quick manner that is professional and pleasing to the person requiring assistance. From time to time there will be those who you can not satisfy just give them a refund and move on. There is no reason to get into arguments and fights with these instead use your time and effort to aid those who appreciate what you do.

A good thing to do in life and business is to treat everyone as you would like them to treat you. People like to be made to feel special and of importance so do your best to do so. At times it is not a bad idea to give out free stuff to clients as a way of thanking them for using your products.

A very great way to aid in your influence with those who are consumers is to have a newsletter that goes out once or twice a week. The newsletter should contain information that is a potential benefit to them and more content than sales pitches. You do need to advise them of things that you have to offer and point out benefits but more as an advisory than an as some huge sales pitch. Make your newsletter informative and refreshing for your list and they will continue to use you. Send them sales pitch after sales pitch and many will ask to be removed from your list and look somewhere else to purchase from.

The better you treat your prospects and consumers the more you will reap now and in the future. Remember that a satisfied customer is one who has no need to look elsewhere for their needs. Your success lies in how people perceive you to be so strive to make the best impression everyday in all your dealings and ventures.

FRONT OFFICE ETIQUETTE

Here are some tips to be followed while at the front office, so as to ensure that every visitor experiences "Delight", whenever they visit your company.

1. *Welcome every visitor with a smile.* A picture paints a thousand words and your body language is very critical. Therefore, you will need to take the time to speak clearly, slowly and in a cheerful and professional voice while greeting every visitor.

2. *Use your normal tone of voice when greeting a visitor.* If you have a tendency to speak loud or shout, avoid doing so while greeting the visitor.
3. *Address the visitor properly by his or her title.* (i.e. Good morning Mr. Vinod, Good afternoon Ms. Kumar, How are you today, Dr.Raj). Never address an unfamiliar visitor by his or her first name.
4. *Do not use poor language.* Respond clearly with "yes" or "no" when speaking. Never use swears words.
5. *Listen to the visitor and what they have to say.* The ability to listen is a problem in general but it is very important to listen to what the visitor has to say. It is always a good habit to repeat the information back to the client when you are taking a message to verify that you have heard and transcribed the message accurately.
6. *Do not eat or drink while you are at the desk.* Only eat or drink during your coffee break or lunch break at the designated place.
7. *Be patient and helpful.* If a visitor is irate or upset, listen to what they have to say and then refer them to the appropriate resource. Never snap back or act rude to the visitor.
8. *Always ask if the visitor has the time to wait.* If you are responsible for handling multiple visitors at once, always ask the visitor politely if you may make them wait. Remember that the visitor could have already waited several minutes in a queue before reaching you may not take lightly to being asked to wait. Once the visitor agrees to wait, follow up with the concerned regularly to ensure that the waiting time is not long.
9. *Always focus on the visitor.* Try not to get distracted by people around you. If someone tries to interrupt

you while you are attending to the visitor, politely remind them that you are attending to the visitor and that you will be with them as soon as you are finished.

10. *Assist visitors while filling out visitor passes.* If your company has a detailed procedure for filling up visitor passes, assist the visitor in the process. It is not advisable to make the visitor spend a lot of time at the front desk filling up the pass, while the time can be utilised by the visitor in a constructive business meeting.
11. *Innovate the visitor pass entry.* Where there is a manual visitor pass register available at the front desk, you can get innovative yourself by implementing methods that will reduce the waiting time at your desk. Alternatively you can also suggest to your management the benefits of automating the visitor pass process. Many such visitor management solutions are available today at competitive prices.

TELEPHONE ETIQUETTE

When it comes to work, you need to think about how you present yourself on the phone and in person. Most of the time you are going to have to make a lot of phone calls regardless. It is the phone call that will make a good impression. If you are too short with them they could think that you aren't a good person to deal with, but if you hold on to them too long, you may end up looking like an idiot. You need to find your medium.

Phone calls are just a part of doing business, but you will want to consider that this is an important part of every business. You will need to learn good techniques for you to have effective conversations.

You first need to make a good first impression. This means that you will answer the phone on the second ring and you need to speak your first words with courtesy and grace. You should always say things like "How may I help You, My name is..." Always watch your tone too. Don't sound like you are dying either. You will want to allow them to think that your day is going perfect even through it's far from perfect. You will want to take an interest in them too, even if you can't help them. Make sure that you ask for their name and how you can direct their call so that they can be the help that they need. Make sure that you are speaking clearly, slowly, and with a lower voice. Don't scream into the phone.

When it comes to putting callers on hold you need to get their permission. This means that you should tell them that you need to get something important in order to help them or transfer them. You will then want to tell them what you are going to do and that it should only be a few moments. People hate waiting, so never leave someone on hold for long periods of time.

If you are answering the phone knowing that someone has been on hold while being transferred you will want to thank them for waiting and then asking them how you can help them. Don't forget that you will have to introduce yourself as soon as you answer the phone. Keep in mind that they may be hostile, depending on how long they have been on hold, you will want to make sure that you do everything you can to assure them that it was an accident and it won't happen again.

As for transferring a call, you will need to tell them that you are transferring them and to hold on. You will also want to tell the person their number incase they get disconnected. You will also want to do this while keeping in mind that people really don't like being pushed to person to person. You need to do this with much poise and respect. It is important for customer service factors that you always show courtesy to the customers. There are a lot of things that you will want to do when it comes to the phone, however, make sure that you think about the first impression that you are giving. You may need to adjust your voice, your volume, or the words that you use when on the phone. Keep in mind that you can't see them and they won't be able to get the nonverbal messages that most people will pick up when talking in person. This means that you will want to say what you mean and mean what you say.

EMAIL ETIQUETTE

Email as a medium of communication has become an almost indispensable tool for business, educational, social and personal purposes. Its importance in the future will, in all likelihood, continue to grow at an almost exponential rate, despite the plague of spam that is choking the internet.

Email has become the standard tool for communication. As a result, many users have developed an informal style of writing for their personal lives. Email has the advantage of regular postal mail in that it is delivered into the recipient's mailbox for them to read and reply to at their convenience, but without the lengthy time delay involved with 'snail mail'. Email also has the advantage of being quick and easy. It doesn't oblige the sender to engage in small-talk with the recipient, as telephones do.

There are no 'official' rules governing electronic communication, though there have been attempts to establish one standard or another as the default, there is no common agreement. So beware people telling you there is one right way, they are assuming too much. As a general rule though, netiquette involves the same principles as plain old etiquette — basic courtesy, respect and ethics.

Understanding email etiquette is an important step in furthering your business. Proper e-mail etiquette is important in anything ranging from e-mailing a cover letter to "casual" correspondence with other profe-ssionals. As more and more opportunities are only found online, the need to develop effective communication skills over e-mail intensifies.

It is amazing to find that in this day and age, some companies have still not realized how important their email communications are. Many companies send email replies late or not at all, or send replies that do not actually answer the questions you asked. If your company is able to deal professionally with email, this will provide your company with that all important competitive edge. Moreover by educating employees as to what can and cannot be said in an email, you can protect your company from awkward liability issues.

A company needs to implement etiquette rules for the following three reasons:

1. *Professionalism*: By using proper email language your company will convey a professional image.
2. *Efficiency*: Emails that get to the point are much more effective than poorly worded emails.
3. *Protection from liability*: employee awareness of email risks will protect your company from costly law suits.

E-mail Etiquette Rules

There are many etiquette guides and many different etiquette rules. Some rules will differ according to the nature of your business and the corporate culture. The most important email etiquette rules that apply to nearly all companies are listed below:

Be concise and to the point

Do not make an e-mail longer than it needs to be. Remember that reading an e-mail is harder than reading printed communications and a long e-mail can be very discouraging to read.

Answer all questions, and pre-empt further questions

An email reply must answer all questions, and pre-empt further questions – If you do not answer all the questions in the original email, you will receive further e-mails regarding the unanswered questions, which will not only waste your time and your customer's time but also cause considerable frustration. Moreover, if you are able to pre-empt relevant questions, your customer will be grateful and impressed with your efficient and thoughtful customer service. Imagine for instance that a customer sends you an email asking which credit cards you accept. Instead of just listing the credit card types, you can guess that their next question will be about how they can order, so you also include some order information and a URL to your order page. Customers will definitely appreciate this.

Use proper spelling, grammar and punctuation

This is not only important because improper spelling, grammar and punctuation give a bad impression of your company, it is also important for conveying the message properly. E-mails with no full stops or commas are difficult to read and can sometimes even change the meaning of the text. And, if your program has a spell checking option, why not use it?

Make it personal

Not only should the e-mail be personally addressed, it

should also include personal i.e. customized content. For this reason auto replies are usually not very effective.

Use templates for frequently used responses

Some questions you get over and over again, such as directions to your office or how to subscribe to your newsletter. Save these texts as response templates and paste these into your message when you need them. You can save your templates in a Word document, or use pre-formatted emails.

Answer swiftly

Customers send an e-mail because they wish to receive a quick response. If they did not want a quick response they would send a letter or a fax. Therefore, each e-mail should be replied to within at least 24 hours, and preferably within the same working day. If the email is complicated, just send an email back saying that you have received it and that you will get back to them. This will put the customer's mind at rest and usually customers will then be very patient!

Do not attach unnecessary files

By sending large attachments you can annoy customers and even bring down their e-mail system. Wherever possible try to compress attachments and only send attachments when they are productive. Moreover, you need to have a good virus scanner in place since your customers will not be very happy if you send them documents full of viruses!

Use proper structure and layout

Since reading from a screen is more difficult than reading

from paper, the structure and lay out is very important for e-mail messages. Use short paragraphs and blank lines between each paragraph. When making points, number them or mark each point as separate to keep the overview.

Do not overuse the high priority option

We all know the story of the boy who cried wolf. If you overuse the high priority option, it will lose its function when you really need it. Moreover, even if a mail has high priority, your message will come across as slightly aggressive if you flag it as 'high priority'.

Do not write in capitals

If you write in capitals it seems as if you are shouting. This can be highly annoying and might trigger an unwanted response in the form of a flame mail. Therefore, try not to send any email text in capitals.

Don't leave out the message thread

When you reply to an email, you must include the original mail in your reply, in other words click 'Reply', instead of 'New Mail'. Some people say that you must remove the previous message since this has already been sent and is therefore unnecessary. If you receive many emails you obviously cannot remember each individual email. This means that a 'threadless email' will not provide enough information and you will have to spend a frustratingly long time to find out the context of the email in order to deal with it. Leaving the thread might take a fraction longer in download time, but it will save the recipient much more time and frustration in looking for the related emails in their inbox!

Add disclaimers to your emails

It is important to add disclaimers to your internal and external mails, since this can help protect your company from liability. Consider the following scenario: an employee accidentally forwards a virus to a customer by email. The customer decides to sue your company for damages. If you add a disclaimer at the bottom of every external mail, saying that the recipient must check each email for viruses and that it cannot be held liable for any transmitted viruses, this will surely be of help to you in court. Another example: an employee sues the company for allowing a racist email to circulate the office. If your company has an email policy in place and adds an email disclaimer to every mail that states that employees are expressly required not to make defamatory statements, you have a good case of proving that the company did everything it could to prevent offensive emails.

Read the email before you send it

A lot of people don't bother to read an email before they send it out, as can be seen from the many spelling and grammar mistakes contained in emails. Apart from this, reading your email through the eyes of the recipient will help you send a more effective message and avoid misunderstandings and inappropriate comments.

Do not overuse reply to all

Only use reply to all if you really need your message to be seen by each person who received the original message.

Mailings use the Bcc: field or do a mail merge

When sending an email mailing, some people place all the email addresses in the To: field. There are two drawbacks to this practice: (1) the recipient knows that you have sent the same message to a large number of recipients, and (2) you are publicising someone else's email address without their permission. One way to get round this is to place all addresses in the Bcc: field. However, the recipient will only see the address from the To: field in their email, so if this was empty, the To: field will be blank and this might look like spamming. You could include the mailing list email address in the To: field, or even better, if you have Microsoft Outlook and Word you can do a mail merge and create one message for each recipient. A mail merge also allows you to use fields in the message so that you can for instance address each recipient personally. For more information on how to do a Word mail merge, consult the Help in Word.

Take care with abbreviations and emoticons

In business emails, try not to use abbreviations such as BTW (by the way) and LOL (laugh out loud). The recipient might not be aware of the meanings of the abbreviations and in business emails these are generally not appropriate. If you are not sure whether your recipient knows what it means, it is better not to use it.

Be careful with formatting

Remember that when you use formatting in your emails, the sender might not be able to view formatting, or might see different fonts than you had intended. When using colours, use a colour that is easy to read on the background.

Take care with rich text and HTML messages

Be aware that when you send an email in rich text or HTML format, the sender might only be able to receive plain text emails. If this is the case, the recipient will receive your message as a .txt attachment. Most email clients however, including Microsoft Outlook, are able to receive HTML and rich text messages.

Do not forward chain letters

Do not forward chain letters. We can safely say that all of them are hoaxes. Just delete the letters as soon as you receive them.

Do not request delivery and read receipts

This will almost always annoy your recipient before he or she has even read your message. Besides, it usually does not work anyway since the recipient could have blocked that function, or his/her software might not support it, so what is the use of using it? If you want to know whether an email was received it is better to ask the recipient to let you know if it was received.

Do not ask to recall a message

Biggest chances are that your message has already been delivered and read. A recall request would look very silly in that case wouldn't it? It is better just to send an email to say that you have made a mistake. This will look much more honest than trying to recall a message.

Do not copy a message or attachment without permission

Do not copy a message or attachment belonging to another user without permission of the originator. If you do not ask permission first, you might be infringing on copyright laws.

Do not use email to discuss confidential information

Sending an email is like sending a postcard. If you don't

want your email to be displayed on a bulletin board, don't send it. Moreover, never make any libelous, sexist or racially discriminating comments in emails, even if they are meant to be a joke.

Use a meaningful subject

Try to use a subject that is meaningful to the recipient as well as yourself. For instance, when you send an email to a company requesting information about a product, it is better to mention the actual name of the product, e.g. 'Product A information' than to just say 'product information' or the company's name in the subject.

Use active instead of passive

Try to use the active voice of a verb wherever possible. For instance, 'We will process your order today', sounds better than 'Your order will be processed today'. The first sounds more personal, whereas the latter, especially when used frequently, sounds unnecessarily formal.

Avoid using urgent and important

Even more so than the high-priority option, you must at all times try to avoid these types of words in an email or subject line. Only use this if it is a really, really urgent or important message.

Avoid long sentences

Try to keep your sentences to a maximum of 15-20 words. Email is meant to be a quick medium and requires a different kind of writing than letters. Also take care not to send emails that are too long. If a person receives an email that looks like a dissertation, chances are that they will not even attempt to read it!

Don't send or forward emails containing libelous, defamatory, offensive, racist or obscene remarks

By sending or even just forwarding one libelous, or offensive remark in an email, you and your company can face court cases resulting in heavy penalties.

Don't forward virus hoaxes and chain letters

If you receive an email message warning you of a new unstoppable virus that will immediately delete everything from your computer, this is most probably a hoax. By forwarding hoaxes you use valuable bandwidth and sometimes virus hoaxes contain viruses themselves, by attaching a so-called file that will stop the dangerous virus. The same goes for chain letters that promise incredible riches or ask your help for a charitable cause. Even if the content seems to be *bona fide,* the senders are usually not. Since it is impossible to find out whether a chain letter is real or not, the best place for it is the recycle bin.

Keep your language gender neutral

In this day and age, avoid using sexist language such as: 'The user should add a signature by configuring his email program'. Apart from using he/she, you can also use the neutral gender: "The user should add a signature by configuring the email program'.

Don't reply to spam

By replying to spam or by unsubscribing, you are confirming that your email address is 'live'. Confirming this will only generate even more spam. Therefore, just hit the delete button or use email software to remove spam automatically.

Use cc: field sparingly

Try not to use the cc: field unless the recipient in the cc: field knows why they are receiving a copy of the message. Using the cc: field can be confusing since the recipients might not know who is supposed to act on the message. Also, when responding to a cc: message, should you include the other recipient in the cc: field as well? This will depend on the situation. In general, do not include the person in the cc: field unless you have a particular reason for wanting this person to see your response. Again, make sure that this person will know why they are receiving a copy.

8

PROVIDING EFFECTIVE INTERNAL CUSTOMER SERVICE

If there are no customers, then there is no business. If there is no business then you do not have a job. It does not even matter if yours is not a customer-facing job. Customers are needed. Question now is how you can look at the situation differently so that providing good service to the customers is something that you can be happy doing. Basic reason, of course, is that you get paid to do the job and providing good customer service is part and parcel of the job. It does help to remind yourself that the organization promptly pays you and it is only fair to deliver your responsibility. Next reason is that good customer service is the best pre-sales effort for the next purchase by the customer. People go all the way out to run promotions and write great copy to entice customers to buy their products. Nothing though can beat good customer service. There are customers who will repeatedly buy from the same company because they are happy with the service provided.

Good customer service is not about falling over yourself providing everything the customer asks for, but it is providing the customer what they rightfully should get for having bought a product from your company.

There is also a completely personal angle that you can look at where service is concerned. Most people nowadays are conscious of their social responsibilities and like to donate or make contributions to worthy causes. Why not make good customer service as such a contribution? In this case, you also get paid for it. The moment you can start thinking that service is something that you want to do, then every customer request will be much easier to respond to.

There will be difficult situations but there will also be customers who will be very appreciative of the service that you provide. For those difficult situations, say to yourself that this is why you are paid a salary and just do it. The moment you stop fighting it, handling the situation gets less difficult. Now, how do you handle difficult situations so that they do not upset you? The best way to handle this is to calmly listen to the customer. Many a time service representatives have a solution even before the problem has been described. Stop to listen first. Then ask clarification questions if necessary before providing the resolution.

Good customer service is not about having a good customer service week once a year. It is about providing good service everyday. As you start work daily, if you can accept that your purpose for being there is to respond to customer needs with concern and a desire to help, it will be a lot easier to get through work. You can even start enjoying it. Remember at a minimum you are getting paid to respond to customer requests. You are also helping to drive more sales from customers because of the excellent service you help provide. Besides this, from a purely personal perspective, you get an opportunity to be of service even without getting out of your normal routine. Start having a different outlook to providing good customer service. It will make a great difference to how you support your customers and importantly to how good you feel deep inside you.

The way you treat your customers will determine if your business is successful or not. If you ship orders late, cannot answer questions about your product, are rude or condescending or you can not update your website regularly, customers will tell their friends and others to avoid your business. But there are ways to make sure your customers are treated with respect without having to sacrifice profits or time.

One of the best ways to provide quality customer service is by creating a website that is easy to navigate. This means that all pages are in logical order, products have full descriptions and order pages are clearly marked. Including contact information is essential to the survival of your business because customers may have questions about their order, products or your website in general.

When customers send email, you should try to answer them within one business day. This will let them know that they are important. If you cannot personally answer the amount of email you are receiving each day and handle other business obligations, you should consider hiring a customer service representative who can take over these duties.

Another way to ensure quality customer service is to make sure that all items shipped are properly wrapped and protected. Items that are thrown into a box without much thought to their safety sends a bad message to customers. Maintaining repeat business is vital to the success of your business. Customers who are pleased with their experiences will purchase other items in the future.

You should always have enough packing and shipping supplies for each day that you send orders. When an order is placed, you should send an email giving the customer an estimate of when it will be shipped and include all shipping information so the customer can track their order. Customers who want to return orders should not be ignored. Make it clear to the customer what the return policy is on your website and on their invoice when they receive the item.

Be patient with customers who want to return an item. Ask them why they were not satisfied and what you can do to help the situation. Many times replacing the item is all the customer will need in order to continue using your website. Customers who are treated poorly will not usually return to make additional purchases.

If you are just starting your business, learning more about ways to help customers find what they are looking for, answering any questions they may have and helping them make returns or exchanges will allow you to develop a reputation for being a quality business from the beginning. If you are patient, considerate and responsive when a problem occurs, you will receive repeat business which will allow your business to continue to grow.

If you own or manage a business, you know how unpleasant many customers can be. Annoying, demanding, critical, dealing with their complaints and irritations can be time-consuming and often prove futile. Yet, customer satisfaction remains an important part of doing a successful job. Happy campers come back and bring others with them, so it's a good idea to satisfy your client base. Plus it's cheaper to maintain current customers than to attract new ones.

1. *Be available.* Frantic customers in search of a human voice rather than an electronic message are relieved and appreciative when you make staff available to answer questions and handle complaints or suggestions. Personal service is a proven method for attracting and keeping a solid client base,

especially in today's hyperactive business world where customers can spend a minute or longer listening to mechanical directions before speaking to a living person. If you must limit a real person's availability to answer calls, consider setting up a Website where customers can email questions and receive prompt replies within 24 hours.

2. *Be courteous.* Even when customers become rude or irate, it is important for your staff to keep calm and remain polite. Train employees to respond to raised voices in calm tones, to critical words with a sympathetic stance. Emphasise customer satisfaction training to prepare your workers to meet the demands of fussy clients and represent the company in the best possible light. Customers who are impressed by your staff's knowledge and patience will become more confident of your company's ability to do a good job.

3. *Be responsive.* Deliver products or services on time. Being late can lead to decreased client trust, and your prize customer may call another firm next time. Initiate a survey to let customers provide feedback that can help to improve your service or products. Show appreciation for customer concerns or suggestions. Deal with complaints promptly and make changes that reflect your concern for the customer's interests.

4. *Offer a good deal at a fair price.* You don't have to charge top quality prices to make a profit. In some cases your effort and subcontracting services may be worth top dollar, but sometimes you don't have to charge the customer an arm and a leg. Provide occasional discounts, throw in a free gift, or take other steps to demonstrate customer appreciation. Shoppers love to feel special, and will come back to your company when you treat them as valued

clients. When possible, it's good business to give customers more than they expect.

5. *Anticipate future customer needs.* In a shifting economy or rapidly evolving industry, a good manager will anticipate his or her clients' needs and make efforts to meet them. Lower prices, a faster gadget, or a more intuitive software programme can make people's lives easier and attract your clients' admiration and repeat business. Don't neglect current company strengths while expanding your product line or enhancing your line of services.

Customer loyalty is important if a business is going to remain solvent or continue to grow. Evaluate your customers' service ratings and evaluate future needs to continue developing a mutually satisfying relationship that will stand the tests of time and competition.

IMPROVING INTERNAL CUSTOMER SERVICE

While companies have allocated a huge budget for the external customer service in order to retain the external customers a little focus is given to the poor internal customer services and their satisfaction. If the internal customer service is not up to standard the effect of this will reach your customers very soon. For improving this, what we need to do is that your internal customer service should be aligned with your company's external focus on customer service.

You might say that this does not matter much. Now to be more precise the internal customer service refers to the services given to your other staff within the organisations in terms of your quality of work environment, communication, motivation, training needs, growth etc.

Here what is required is your appropriate action in understanding their issues, how well you understand their training needs in whatever work they are doing. How well you are trying to solve the problems of your staff. Furthermore, how much ease the staff feel in directly communicating the issues or concerns to the management for its timely resolution. Sometimes the staff might not bring their issues or concerns into your attention due to one reason or the other, which will eventually result in creation of a big problem which could have easily be resolved if it would have been communicated to you earlier.

In corporate culture as a head of a company you will find yourself to be in middle of wars between different departments. Marketing fighting with Finance, cursing marketing, sales blaming customer service and the list of rivalry goes on. What we need to do it is to have a common platform and rapid and constant communication with all concerned to keep everyone on the same page. Basically, we are all concerned about the finished product. But at subjective level we have our apprehensions.

First we have to resolve the internal disputes and create and win-win situation for everyone. We can do this by creating responsiveness, effective organisational communication, transparency, and a visualisation of fulfilment of internal customer service.

Now how to align the internal customer service with the external customer service here are some guidelines.

- — Employees should have sufficient knowledge of what they are explaining to the customer in professional manner, if this is not done it will give an amateurish impression of your organisation and customer will lose confidence in your company and its product and services.

— Employees should never pass on the blame within the organisation to some other department's employees. This will give an impression that the internal staff is not getting along each other.

— Employees from different departments should be given an opportunity to build bridges between each other through cross trainings, joint gatherings and parties etc.

— If there is an issue which involves delay. Then, the concerned department should have proper communication about the time frame of the issue resolution and what are the reasons of holdup. Sometimes the departments might think that it's not relevant to reveal any information. But on the contrary it is vital that all the concerned should have basic idea about the problem so they could guide the customer accordingly with confidence.

— Effective motivational techniques should be employed for the satisfaction of the internal employees which will intern leave ripple effect in provision of the extra ordinary external customer service.

Now if we consider paying sufficient attention to the internal customer service then would defiantly provide the best possible external customer service.

Professionals have to realise that they are just as accountable to their internal customers as they are to the traditional ones. Alienating your internal customers result in a soured opinion of not only the individual, but the entire staff of the offender. Human resources is a perfect example of an element of businesses that has many internal customers that they work with. Their customers include managers, executives and every other employee. Treating every customer with respect, professionalism and courtesy is paramount to establishing relationships and an excellent reputation.

Every leader needs to ensure that their people appreciate that customer service matters to even the internal customers. People expect respect, professionalism, and understanding when working with co-workers. If leaders allow their employees to alienate one another they are failing as leaders—it will not be long before the quality employees of an infected organisation start walking out the door.

While companies focus thousands of rupees on external customer service in hopes of wooing and retaining customers, little attention is being paid to the effect poor internal customer service has on customer satisfaction. It all starts within your organisation! Sooner or later the ripple effect reaches your customers. To really walk your service talk, make sure your commitment to internal customer service matches your company's external focus on customer care.

When we think of customer service we think of staff serving customers over a counter or over the phone. But customer service occurs within your organisation as well. How well is your staff serving its internal customers: other departments, its management, vendors and consultants? Believe it or not, it all counts. Internal customer service refers to service directed to others within your organisation. It refers to your level of responsiveness, quality, communication, teamwork and morale.

Good internal customer service starts with good morale within your group. Are your people happy? Do they feel good about themselves and their contributions to the goals of the department and to the company at large? They should, and effort should be made to help them do so. Happy employees are productive, and customers take note. Happy employees are also better team players. Will you fly the airline whose employees are striking with management, or the airline whose employees are management? Employees invested in employee stock purchasing plans with matching contributions see themselves as much more a part of the company. Thus, as the company goes, so do they go.

Many organisational charts employ an inverted pyramid with customers at top. Some companies instead put their employees at the top. In many senses, the employees are management's customers. Corporate values that emphasise treating employees well translate to good customer care too. Does your organisation value its people? Invariably, companies that care about their people can better ask their people to care about their customers.

Catering to Customer Service Needs

Here are five tips for your organisation to help strengthen its internal customer service orientation.

— Employees should never complain within earshot of customers. It gives them the impression your company isn't well run, shaking their confidence in you.

— Employees should never complain to customers about other department's employees. Who wants to patronise a company whose people don't get along with each other.

— Employees at every level should strive to build bridges between departments. This can be done through cross training, joint picnics, parties or offsites, or creative gatherings, as well as day-to-day niceties.

— Utilise post mortems after joint projects so everyone can learn from the experience. Fences can be mended and new understandings gleaned when everyone reviews what went right or wrong. By doing do after the project the immediate pressure is off, yet stronger bonds can be forged while the experience is fresh in peoples' minds. Not doing so can result in lingering animosities that will exacerbate future collaborations.

— Consider letting your employees become "Customer for a Day" to experience firsthand what your customers experience when doing business with you.

By improving internal customer service you have just enhanced the customer service your external customers receive.

How to Provide Quality Customer Service

In the marketing world, a brand is so much more than a mere logo or symbol. It is the intangible sum of a product's attributes: its name, packaging price, history, reputation, and customer experience. It represents every touchpoint in a company or organisation. Every individual that encounters a customer or client can make (or break) the brand.

Quality customer service means going beyond what's expected, adding value to the customer experience. When you under-promise and over-deliver, your customers will come back, rave about you, tell others, and be your best friend—as long as this behaviour and attitude is consistent.

Quality is a customer determination based upon a customer's actual experience with a product or service, measured against his or her requirements—stated or unstated, conscious or merely sensed, technically operational or entirely subjective—and always representing a moving target in a competitive market.

When you provide quality customer service, you help connect the dots for your company' or organisation's brand. It's part of your brand promise, stated or not. Meeting or exceeding your customers' expectations gives your company credibility and helps build its reputation in your market.

You have a better chance of retaining your customers for the long term, as well as keeping your employees engaged and committed. Imagine a workplace where service is not strongly valued or is inconsistent. It must be challenging to retain employees who are at the receiving end of incessant verbal abuse from malcontents and dissatisfied customers.

Another important reason to provide quality customer service answers the "What's in it for me?" question, which is not always verbalised by some employees. Good customer service helps generate more revenue, which enables the company or organisation to live its mission.

The end result from an internal perspective? More money begets more mission, which begets growth and innovation, which begets increased salaries, bonuses and/or promotions, which begets happy employees, happy customers, and so on, and so on... as the old shampoo commercial says. When the wheels turn efficiently, and customers and employees are content, the "corporate" environment is ripe for the brand to flourish.

Whether your company or organisation is large or small, providing good customer service begins with the internal environment. Employee satisfaction, customer loyalty, and profitability are interconnected. Anyone who plays a role in your organisation in producing or supporting your end product or service is part of the internal process—from those answering the phone, cleaning your bathrooms, supplying your office products, sorting your mail and fixing your computer, to the president or CEO and board of directors (for corporations and nonprofits). Each one plays a role in the never ending chain of activity that transpires daily. When one link in the chain breaks or falters, it can affect the entire chain.

CUSTOMER SERVICE STANDARDS

If you have existing internal customer service standards or protocols, it may be time to see whether they're still meeting your needs. If technology has changed the way you do things, and your manuals haven't kept up, it's time for a revision. If the existing standards focus solely on external customers, adding a separate section for this purpose will show a commitment on management's part to improve your internal protocols. It should help build morale and encourage a more cooperative workplace. If you were starting from scratch, it would help to identify current weaknesses and gaps before developing new internal customer service standards.

Employees often confer in the lunchroom, bathroom, nearby coffee shop or conference room. Office or workplace chatter is a reality, and most of us have been part of it at some point in our careers. Sometimes, the idle workplace gossip is a channel for employees to socialise, share information and connect with each other. After all, when you spend half or more of your waking hours in the workplace, it becomes your home away from home, and your workplace friends become your pseudo-family.

However, if the gossip is widespread or frequent, and is the result of workplace tension, boredom, or demoralisation, there's a larger issue at stake besides your customer service needs. It might mean that your company requires a cultural overhaul. Sometimes, being more transparent from the top and developing better internal communication with employees can solve the problem.

The more informed they are, the less anxiety and greater sense of comfort they experience.

In extreme circumstances, the environment may be toxic or very negative, with employees on their guard, feeling tense and uneasy. This environment often has a high staff turnover and absentee rate. It's ripe for internal sabotage of conflicting goals and objectives, a disaster for the mission or bottom line. It would be a waste of time developing internal customer service standards in a workplace such as this, when the corporate culture is dysfunctional. It would be like icing a cake made of hardened sawdust. It may look good on the outside, but once you cut into it, crumbles.

No amount of superficial remedies can correct a poor corporate culture. It requires examination of the root cause and changing things from there. Bringing in outsourced specialists to analyse, make recommendations and conduct staff training often helps to reconfigure attitudes and build trust.

STRENGTHENING INTERNAL CUSTOMER SERVICE

When your workplace is ripe for improving internal customer service, begin with market research. The more you learn about existing gaps and shortcomings, the better you'll be able to correct the situation. Understanding internal customers' needs, frustrations, and challenges give managers the opportunity to make improvements and increase performance and employee satisfaction.

Enlist the assistance of your internal human resources executive or outsourced professionals to develop a staff survey and research methodology. If budgets are tight, develop a cross-department staff committee to work on this. It's especially valuable when the staff owns this process.

Communicate with the staff, outlining what your objectives are. As part of the survey, ask staff to give examples of desired outcomes. When you provide quality internal customer service, how will staff members conduct themselves and what will the workplace look like as a result? Here are some examples of possible desired outcomes:

— When a deadline is imminent, or a problem requires solving, staff members can ask for assistance from another department or staff person, and they will work together or brainstorm as a team.

— Employees do not complain to customers about other employees or departments.

— Employees' opinions are valued and they are empowered to make decisions.

— The company recognises and rewards employees who exemplify quality customer-service behaviours.

Keep your staff informed on the progress of this process. The more empowered staff are, the more engaged they will be in making changes. When results are evaluated and new protocols and behaviors are established, it helps to put it in writing in the form of a manual or policy. Following up with staff training ensures longer-term results and should incorporate the rationale behind quality internal customer service, as it relates to the company brand.

When employees understand the big picture of the company's vision, and the role they can play in achieving that goal, there's a greater likelihood that they'll be team-oriented. Internal communication is imperative for keeping employees informed, not only of the latest company policies but also of the organisation's strategies.

As part of staff orientation, it's important for management to impart the company's mission and vision. When each department leader prepares a presentation for new staff members on the roles and responsibilities of their areas of focus, it gives the staff an opportunity to ask questions and understand how each cog contributes to the overall result.

Follow this up with internal newsletters or open forums to allow departments to share their successes or keep other staff informed of their efforts. For companies and organisations in one location, this can take the form of monthly lunchtime presentations. For larger organisations in multiple locations, the corporate intranet and staff newsletters can fulfil this purpose.

Though time is a luxury, it's important for senior staff to visit periodically with other departments and office locations, not only to show the face behind the title but also to keep the lines of communication open. This time can be tacked on to another purpose for cost savings, and incorporated into staff training in the executive's area of expertise.

9

EFFECTIVE CUSTOMER HANDLING

There is a difference between dissatisfied or disgruntled customers and complainers. The former often only have to answer to themselves; the latter most likely will have to answer to others about the results of their experience. Everyone has dissatisfied or disgruntled and complaining customers and clients. Businesses have them, organisations have them, government certainly has them, and, unfortunately both employees and employers have them. Anyone offering ideas, information, skills, services or products has obligations:

1. The first obligation is to what is being offered – to make sure that what is being offered is presented in the best possible manner, given the limitations of time, space, effort, and/or money. These limitations should not be used as excuses for a poor presentation.
2. The second obligation is to give customers enough choices so they believe that in making their decision to buy or not they have made the best decision. If customers sense they are not being given enough options, they will delay their decision until they find the right options to satisfy their

needs. This is called giving customers a "marketplace," a place where they see what their options are. A marketplace can be in time, location, space, size, colour, material, effort, services, or money. There are almost 100 ways to make a marketplace.

3. The third obligation is to make sure one's customers are never embarrassed for accepting or, even, contemplating accepting what is offered. If a customer thinks they will be embarrassed for buying or even contemplating buying or accepting what is offered that they will not bring it before their family, friends, associates, acquaintances, customers/clients. Often this is because the business did not give the customer the information necessary to use in their presentation when relating their experience. The result may be that the customer will badmouth the business, the business's presentation and the products much to the detriment of the business and the business's products.

Conversely, customers have three obligations,

1. To pay for what was received as agreed in time, space, effort, and/or money.
2. To expect, and possibly demand, that everything be presented in its best possible manner.
3. To complain if they don't like the way they were treated or the way something was presented.

When a Customer comes in to complain, they are exercising their obligation to whomever is offering the idea, information, skill, service or product. When an employee receives a complaint from their supervisor, the supervisor is exercising their obligation to the employee. When management receives a complaint from their employee, the employee is exercising their obligation to their management.

No one likes complaints. If a business doesn't have complaints, it's not doing anything . . . and that will bring on the complaint from someone that the business isn't doing anything. An adage is, every business deserves the customers they have. By this, it is meant that when one has a demanding customer one has to understand why that person is so demanding. There could be many reasons:

1. The customer does not believe they are getting "added-value" — they want to get more than they are paying for or, as with a complainer, they want to pay less, i.e., complaining with the idea that they will get their money back.
2. They have a problem, they are being challenged by someone else and in order to come up with an answer to alleviate the problem they will be take that problem back to the seller. This is known as the-squeaky-wheel-that-gets-the-grease syndrome.
3. They have been sent on a mission to come back with the "right" and they believe something or someone is getting in the way. Hence, they will be "punished" i.e. embarrassed for not having the information wanted.
4. It could be that they had "buyer's remorse" in that they could not justify their purchase without getting something additional from the seller that would give them the "power" to justify the purchase.

When people find that their or others' complaints are not met, they will get even in any way they can. This could be to come in and yell where others can hear them, delay paying or not paying, telling others their side but not the seller's side, of the problem, story, etc. There are many ways to handle complaints. The first thing is to let them know that not only are you listening to them, you are writing down what they are saying as they are saying it because they see you do it, and that you want them to repeat the complaint several times so you know you have it right.

If a customer keeps calling about trivial things it may be due to any of the above or it may be that doing so makes them feel that, by doing so, they are letting you know that they have confidence that you will not steer them wrong. It may be that calling you makes them feel that they are an important customer even if you don't think so. While disgruntled customers may not fit this term, certainly complainers are often called "customers from hell." Customers from hell are those that do not come in but tell hundreds of others that you are a vendor from hell. When that happens you may both meet in the same place.

Handling complaints can be outline in four steps:

1. Make sure the complainer is sitting down. If left standing when the recipient of the complaint in interrupted or goes to look up some records the complainer will become impatient or just leave the situation. Sitting in a chair can be tantamount to having the Customer glued to the chair.
2. If possible, do not put a table, counter, or desk between the complainer and the person receiving the complaint. Doing so makes it adversarial. Selling is a partnership – and the listener before, during and after the hearing the problem is the complainer's liaison to the organisation or business. Of the customer senses that their time, effort, space or effort is being wasted, it can acerbate the

problem. When one's Customer/partner has a problem, guess who has the problem?

3. Get out a pad and pencil, ask the complainer to state the problem. Write down what they are saying as they are saying it. This has two different effects on the situation. First, the Customer's complaint is intangible until it is put down in tangible form. By writing down all the particulars of the complaint it becomes tangible. Secondly, since the listener cannot write as fast as the complainer talks, the complainer while waiting for the writer to catch up will be slowing down their presentation, hence causing a calming effect.
4. Get the Customer to repeat the story as many times as possible and note each change in the story. Each time, more pertinent information will come out.
5. Very often, the complainer has been told what to say by someone else. It is their sales presentation. The person receiving the complaint is the buyer and will not buy the validity of the complaint unless they can sell the validity to someone else.
6. Many complaints stem from the fact that the customer was not given, in tangible form, the answers to questions they needed to answer the questions before the question(s) were asked.

Process the complaint as soon as possible. Let the customer know when they will be getting a reply and get back to them before that time. If the service or Products is defective, do not argue! Make it right, away. Do not hesitate to replace it, do it over, or give a refund. If the reply is negative to what the complainer wants, the negative reply has to be sold to whomever the dissatisfied or disgruntled or complaining customer will be talking to. Lastly, it is everyone's obligation within their working or familiar environment where the problem arose to discuss the problem, the situation and the solution. This information will help others handle the problems later.

CUSTOMER SERVICE TIPS

In retail, it's inevitable that there will be the occasional disgruntled customer. No matter how wonderful your products are or how committed you are to provide the best customer service, problems do occur. Armed with the following customer service tips, you can diffuse a situation and possibly even save the customer, as well as the sale.

Stay Calm

When a customer is upset, remember that it is not a personal attack. Let them talk as long as they need to, not only to get it off their chest, but to thoroughly explain the problem. Listen carefully! You cannot fix what you don't understand, so be sure to ask the customer enough questions to learn what is bothering them. By simply listening, the customer will realise that you are interested in their problem and he/she will eventually calm down enough to discuss the situation in a positive manner.

Apologise

Once you understand why the customer is upset, apologise. Even if you don't agree with their complaint, you are at least letting them know you validate them and will work towards a resolution. This also separates the emotion from the problem. As a general rule, the expression of empathy to the customer should come right after the apology. When you feel you fully understand, restate your understanding of the problem at hand.

Resolve Their Problem

Your business should have policies in place to prepare people working the front lines to deal with customer service issues. However, not all situations are the same and therefore not all remedies should be the same either. If the disgruntled customer has made it clear what will satisfy him, then do everything within your power to accommodate that customer. This shows your commitment to resolving their problem.

Follow Up

Whatever promises you make to the customer to resolve the issue, be sure to follow up. Call when you said you would call. Even if you don't have the resolution, let the customer know you're sticking to your word. This shows the customer that his/her business is important to you and you're actively working towards getting things fixed.

Learn From Mistakes

Dealing with each unpleasant customer should be a learning experience. Customer feedback should be viewed as an opportunity for change. Keep in mind that not all customers can be pleased. Some people are just complainers and nothing you do will change that. But everything you can correct about this situation will help with future events. Keep improving in areas over which you have control.

Even though the customer is upset, this is still a sale. He or she has already made a purchase and you have their money, so make sure your response is timely and respectful. Customers with complaints simply want you to be aware of the problem and take the necessary steps to correct it. Sometimes there are no substitutions, discounts or freebies you can offer that will keep the sale. Although you may lose this purchase, the attempts you've made to win over the customer may help retain future sales.

How to Deal with Angry Customers

Angry and difficult customers are a challenge that every entrepreneur will face. When your time comes, will you be ready?. Small business owners know that angry customers are an unavoidable part of doing business. Sooner or later, you are going to encounter people who are not happy about some aspect of their relationship with your company. But an angry customer isn't necessarily a former customer. In fact, the majority of angry customers will continue to do business with you, especially if you go the extra step to provide a satisfactory resolution to their problem. Here are some simple things you can do to train your staff to deal with angry customers and keep them coming back for years to come.

Resolve the Problem Quickly

No one likes to be ignored, particularly if they have a problem. The worst thing you can do when dealing with angry customers is to put off their complaint or send them on a wild goose chase to find someone who will help them. Respond promptly to their concerns and let them know that helping them is your top priority.

Don't Take It Personally

Emotions run high in situations involving irate customers. Even though the problem may have been out of your control, the customer will likely focus his frustration toward an employee because at that moment the employee represents the company. Avoid the temptation to take the complaint personally. Instead, try to diffuse the emotion of the moment by remaining calm and responding in a reasonable manner.

Admit Your Mistakes

If you or a member of your staff has made a mistake, admit it. Nothing gets accomplished by trying to maintain the appearance of perfection. The customer just gets more frustrated and angry than they already are. Sometimes simply admitting a mistake will be enough to satisfy the customer and resolve the problem.

Be Nice, But Firm

It's good business to always maintain an attitude of courtesy and respect toward your customers, even when they are treating you badly. But being nice doesn't mean that you have to always give in, either. Instruct your employees how to be polite to difficult customers while being firm about your company's policies.

Support Your Employees

Your employees need to know that you will stand behind them when they are placed in the difficult position of dealing with an irritated customer. Nothing is more demoralising for an employee than watching their employer take the customer's side against them, especially if they are enforcing the policies you have laid down for them.

Make a Peace Offering

If all else fails, make a peace offering in the form of a

minor concession or free merchandise. This doesn't have to be expensive. For example, when restaurants encounter angry patrons it's not unusual for them to offer a free dessert or appetiser to diffuse the situation. The majority of angry customers just want to feel valued. A peace offering communicates that they are important to you and that you are willing to do what it takes make things right.

Handling Challenging Situations

Most Customer Service Professionals deal with many challenging customer situations. These situations may include:

1. A customer who is upset about the quality or delivery of our product/service.
2. A product return or a cancellation of services.
3. Incorrect information given to the customer.
4. A customer who is negative toward your company due to past experiences.
5. Confrontational issues and conflict.
6. Angry customers.
7. Explaining a company policy or procedure.
8. Fielding a request to escalate a call to management.

The ultimate goal in these challenging situations is to provide a win-win solution. We want our customer to leave the interaction feeling listened to, well taken care of, and valued. A customer-focused mindset will have a tremendous impact on accomplishing these goals. Along with customer focus, an invaluable tool for dealing with challenging situations is the Five-Step Process.

Five-Step Process

Have you ever been an upset customer, calling your

product or service provider with a serious problem? If you receive a satisfactory resolution AND you feel listened to, well taken care of, and valued during your interaction, aren't you likely to consider doing business with this company again? The Five-Step Process will help us to provide our customers with this positive experience. Aside from reaching a win-win solution, the goal of the Five-Step Process is to leave our customers feeling listened to, well taken care of, and valued. Let's examine the specific steps of the Five-Step Process.

1. *Strategise*

How do you develop a strategy?

1. Develop your goal for the interaction. What do you want as the end result?
2. Identify your parameters: what can you do or provide the customer independently or with your supervisor's approval? What can't you do because of policy or business reasons?
3. Prepare by identifying common problems and win-win solutions.

Your strategy should be to arrive at a solution that will be a win for both your company and the customer. If you are successful, you will retain the customer, exceed the customer's expectations, and provide a very positive customer experience so that he/she will want to continue doing business with your company.

2. *Acknowledge*

The acknowledgement is essential to communicating in challenging situations. Use phrases like, "I understand how you feel", "I see", "I apologise", "I am sorry", "I can see how you might feel that way" so that customers feel that they have been heard and that we respect them. It clears the way for us to move forward by helping diffuse the emotion and placing us on the side of the customer.

3. Clarify

Sometimes we mistakenly proceed to resolve a problem based on what we think the customer was saying. This third step of the process allows us to clarify and draw out information to make sure that we understand the customer's true concern.

4. Present Resolution

The fourth step is to present a resolution. Presenting a resolution is not a challenge if we've done the first three steps properly. As we present the resolution, we want to state specifically what we are going to do for the customer. We may also offer alternatives.

5. Checkback

The checkback is our opportunity to make sure that the customer is satisfied and feels good about the resolution. Examples of checkbacks include:

1. "How does that sound?"
2. "What do you think about x?"
3. "Are you with me?"
4. "Does that make sense?"
5. "Will that meet your needs?"
6. "Would that be satisfactory?"

Using the Five-Step Process

The following example illustrates a customer-focused approach, applying the Five-Step Process.

1. *Strategise*: Our strategy is to retain the customer whenever possible. We want to provide the customer with a positive experience while balancing both the business and customer needs. We don't want to simply accept return merchandise since we know we will lose the customer. A customer calls to complain about the quality of the product he received.
2. *Acknowledge*: "I apologise that the product was not of the quality that you expected. I understand your frustration. I can help."
3. *Clarify*: "In order for us to improve on the quality – and for me to better serve you, may I ask what specific areas were of poor quality?"
4. *Present Resolution*: "We would be happy to exchange the product for a similar product of higher quality."
5. *Checkback*: "Would that be satisfactory?"

Depending on the customer's responses, we may actually have to go through the Five-Step Process many times during one customer interaction. The Five-Step Process will help you to avoid becoming argumentative by lessening the conflict and opening dialogue with the customer. It will assist you in providing a more positive customer experience.

HANDLING CUSTOMER COMPLAINTS

Handling customer complaints can be difficult, but successful organisations rely on satisfied customers. Customers are increasingly demanding the best, fastest and most convenient and if they feel their complaint or objection is not being heard and dealt with effectively they will take their custom elsewhere. Being able to listen, respond to and handle customer complaints in a positive manner will be an important step in creating long-term customer loyalty.

This practical and interactive handling customer complaints training course will help develop the range of professional interpersonal and communication skills required to deal with customer complaints confidently. Practical examples, role-plays, self-appraisals and discussion forums are used to enable delegates to develop the skills to 'think on their feet' and leave the customer reassured.

Objectives

1. Gather information, even in a tense situation, in order to deal with the real problem.
2. Defuse customer anger and build rapport.
3. Communicate with confidence and assurance.
4. Maintain professionalism under pressure.
5. Create customer satisfaction.
6. Provide a solution.
7. Monitor and analyse complaint levels and identify remedial action.

Content of Course

The Complaint—How to Control It?

1. The damage complaints can do to your organisation
2. Making sure the complaint does not escalate
3. Accepting customer feedback graciously
4. Rebuilding the customer relationship

The various techniques required to handle written, telephone and face-to-face complaints

Communication that Works

1. Developing the right attitude—feeling good, thinking positively.
2. How to sound confident, caring and helpful—building rapport.
3. Active listening.
4. Gathering the information.
5. Checking understanding.
6. Successful telephone techniques—the do's and don'ts.

Remaining Calm—Not Overreacting

1. Recognising how serious is the customer's concern.
2. Defusing a difficult situation.
3. Empathise with the complaint—don't join in the criticism.
4. Gaining the customer's respect.
5. Identifying common ground.

Creating Satisfaction

1. Ensuring the customer feels listened to.
2. Let the customer know what can/will be done about their complaint.
3. Taking responsibility for the successful outcome.
4. Getting across your point of view—rebuilding commitment.

5. Monitoring complaint levels versus performance standards.
6. Identifying processes to deal with the most common objections.
7. Influencing the organisation—collectively looking to avoid future problems.

10

MANAGE YOUR CUSTOMER CARE

Customer care involves putting systems in place to maximise your customers' satisfaction with your business. It should be a prime consideration for every business—your sales and profitability depends on keeping your customers happy. Customer care is more directly important in some roles than others. For receptionists, sales staff and other employees in customer-facing roles, customer care should be a core element of their job description and training, and a core criterion when you're recruiting.

But don't neglect the importance of customer care in other areas of your business. For instance, your warehousing and dispatch departments may have minimal contact with your customers—but their performance when fulfilling orders has a major impact on customers' satisfaction with your business.

A huge range of factors can contribute to customer satisfaction, but your customers—both consumers and other businesses—are likely to take into account:

1. How well your product or service matches customer needs,
2. The value for money you offer,
3. Your efficiency and reliability in fulfilling orders,

4. The professionalism, friendliness and expertise of your employees,
5. How well you keep your customers informed,
6. The after-sales service you provide.

In business-to-business trading, providing a high level of customer care often requires you to find out what your customers want. Once you have identified your most valuable customers or best potential customers, you can target your highest levels of customer care towards them. Another approach, particularly in the consumer market, is the obligation to treat all consumers to the highest standard.

COLLECT CUSTOMER INFORMATION

Information about your customers and what they want is available from many sources, including:

1. Their order history,
2. Records of their contacts with your business—phone calls, meetings and so on,
3. Direct feedback—if you ask them, customers will usually tell you what they want,
4. Changes in individual customers' order patterns,
5. Changes in the overall success of specific products or services,
6. Feedback about your existing range—what it does and doesn't do,
7. Enquiries about possible new products or services,
8. Feedback from your customers about things they buy from other businesses,
9. Changes in the goods and services your competitors are selling,

10. Feedback and referrals from other, non-competitive suppliers.

Manage Your Information

It's important that you draw up a plan about how customer information is to be gathered and used in your business. Establish a customer-care policy. Assign a senior manager as the policy's champion but make sure that all your staff are involved—often the lower down the scale you go, the more direct contact with customers there is.

Measure Your Customer Service Levels

Where possible, put systems in place to assess your performance in business areas which significantly affect your customers' satisfaction levels. Identify Key Performance Indicators (KPIs) which reflect how well you're responding to your customers' expectations.

For instance, you might track:

1. Sales renewal rates,
2. The number of queries or complaints about your products or services,
3. The number of complaints about your employees,
4. The number of damaged or faulty goods returned
5. Average order-fulfilment times,
6. The number of contacts with a customer each month,
7. The volume of marketing material sent out and responses generated,
8. Time taken from order to delivery.

Your customers and employees will be useful sources of information about the KPIs which best reflect key customer service areas in your business. Make sure the things you measure are driven not by how your business currently runs, but by how your customers would like to see it run. There are important areas of customer service which are more difficult to measure.

Many of these are human factors such as a receptionist's telephone manner or a salesperson's conduct while visiting clients. In these areas it's crucial that you get feedback from your customers about their perceptions of your customer service. Customer surveys, feedback programmes and occasional phone calls to key customers can be useful ways of gauging how customer service levels in your business are perceived.

Customer Feedback and Contact Programmes

Customer feedback and contact programmes are two ways of increasing communication with your customers. They can represent great opportunities to listen to your customers and to let them know more about what you can offer. Customer feedback can provide you with detailed information about how your business is perceived. It's a chance for customers to voice objections, suggest changes or endorse your existing processes, and for you to listen to what they say and act upon it.

Feedback is most often gathered using questionnaires, in person, over the telephone or by post. The purpose of customer contact programmes is to help you deliver tailored information to your customers. One example is news of a special offer that is relevant to a past purchase—another is a reminder sent at the time of year when a customer traditionally places an order. Contact programmes are particularly useful for reactivating relationships with lapsed customers.

Do your best to make sure that your customers feel the extra contact is relevant and beneficial to them—

bombarding customers with unwanted calls or marketing material can be counter-productive. Newsletters and email bulletins allow you to keep in touch with useful information.

Customer Loyalty Schemes

While good overall service is the best way of generating customer loyalty, sometimes new relationships can be strengthened, or old ones refreshed, using customer loyalty schemes. These are programmes that use fixed or percentage discounts, extra goods or prizes to reward customers for behaviour that benefits your business. They can also be used to persuade customers to give you another try if you feel you have successfully tackled past problems with your customer service.

You can decide to offer rewards on the basis of:

1. Repeat custom,
2. Cumulative spend,
3. Orders for large quantities or with a high value,
4. Prompt payment,
5. Length of relationship.

For example, a car wash might offer free cleaning every tenth visit or a free product if a customer opts for the deluxe service. A mail-order company might seek to revive the interest of lapsed customers by offering a voucher redeemable against purchases—response rates with such vouchers can be improved by setting an expiry date.

You can also provide key customers with loyalty cards that entitle them to a discount on all their purchases. Employees who deal with customers' orders should be fully aware of current offers and keep customers informed. Sometimes brochures and other marketing materials are the best way of getting word out about a new customer incentive. Don't forget though that your customers' view of the overall service you provide will influence their loyalty much more than short-term rewards will.

Use Customer Care

Your existing customers are among the most important assets of your business—they have already chosen you instead of your competitors. Keeping their custom costs far less than attracting new business, so it's worth taking steps to make sure that they're satisfied with the service they receive.

There are a number of techniques you can employ, including:

1. Providing a free customer helpline,
2. Answering frequently asked questions on your website,
3. Following up sales with a courtesy call,
4. Providing free products that will help customers look after or make the most of their purchases,
5. Sending reminders when services or check-ups are due,
6. Offering preferential discounts to existing customers on further purchases.

Existing customer relationships are opportunities to increase sales because your customers will already have a degree of trust in your recommendations. Cross-selling and up-selling are ways of increasing either the range or the value of what you sell by pointing out new purchase possibilities to these customers. Alerting customers when new, upgraded or complimentary products become available—perhaps through regular emails or newsletters—is one way of increasing sales.

To retain your customers' trust, however, never try to sell them something that clearly doesn't meet their needs. Remember, your aim is to build a solid long-term relationship with your customers rather than to make quick one-off profits. Satisfied customers will contribute to your business for years, through their purchases and through recommendations and referrals of your business.

Dealing with Customer Complaints

Every business has to deal with situations in which things go wrong from a customer's point of view. However you respond if this happens, don't be dismissive of your customer's problem—even if you're convinced you're not at fault. Although it might seem contradictory, a customer with a complaint represents a genuine opportunity for your business:

1. If you handle the complaint successfully, your customer is likely to prove more loyal than if nothing had gone wrong,
2. People willing to complain are rare—your complaining customer may be alerting you to a problem experienced by many others who silently took their custom elsewhere,

Complaints should be handled courteously, sympat—hetically and—above all—swiftly. Make sure that your business has an established procedure for dealing with customer complaints and that it is known to all your employees. At the very least it should involve:

1. Listening sympathetically to establish the details of the complaint,
2. Recording the details together with relevant material, such as a sales receipt or damaged goods,
3. Offering rectification—whether by repair, replacement or refund,

4. Appropriate follow-up action, such as a letter of apology or a phone call to make sure that the problem has been made good.

If you're proud of the way you rectify problems—by offering no-questions refunds, for example—make sure your customers know about it. Your method of dealing with customer problems is one more way to stay ahead of your competitors.

CUSTOMER CARE SOLUTION

Achieving the highest quality customer service is an exercise in vigilance. Having the best people, cutting-edge technology and time-tested protocols is certainly helpful. True excellence, however, is not simply a one-time event. It requires a continuous process. What is the best way to secure and use customer information to improve customer service and learn more about every interaction with customers? Also, how do you guarantee that the customer feedback is accurate and not biased?

Surveys are one of the best methods to secure customer information, but many times, surveys are either biased or skewed to the negative because many customers complete surveys only if they have had a bad experience. Although these negative surveys are helpful, they do not paint a complete picture of the situation or provide accurate data to use and react to.

Additionally, most surveys typically take time to compile, and by the time the company receives the data, the time frame to react has already passed, and a solution, if necessary, might not work in the long-term. When selecting a survey tool for your customer service representatives and call centre agents, the most important features to consider for best-practice results are as follows:

1. Agent anonymous. By being "agent anonymous," the tool should ensure that the agent cannot influence or bias the survey in any way through voice inflections or changes in service based on the caller's interest in taking the survey. The IVR, not the agent, should ask the caller if he or she would like to participate in the survey.
2. Interactive. Interactivity makes the survey easy and therefore more likely to be completed.
3. Time-efficient. Customer surveys are important, but the customer's time is even more important. Keeping surveys short will increase the number of participants as well as the validity of the survey results.
4. Qualitative and quantitative results. Numbers and ratings can provide only so much information. Hearing the actual customer voice allows that individual to share his or her true feelings; the tone of voice and specific words used will ultimately allow a complete understanding of the customer's sentiments.
5. Real-time access to results. Staying on top of the information allows managers to react quickly and adjust methods as necessary. In an age of information, data that are a week old can be worthless since needs and direction can change very quickly.

West Interactive recently introduced the Insight Customer Intelligence survey system, a solution that allows contact centers to implement a network-based, real-time automated customer survey tool to measure the quality of customer interactions and improve customer retention. Insight Customer Intelligence is completely agent anonymous. It is customisable with customer satisfaction ratings, including spoken comments, with 100 per cent recording of the agent call and customer responses.

Based on the customer's satisfaction score, Insight can also dynamically request if the customer would like a callback or needs to be transferred for immediate assistance. Call center managers can see the results in a real-time Internet dashboard, allowing managers and supervisors to react immediately to agent issues.

Customer satisfaction may seem easy to understand, but it is often difficult to define and even more difficult to measure. With Insight Customer Intelligence, companies can learn more about what matters most: their customers. Boosting customer satisfaction can translate into additional revenue per customer, improved customer retention, reduced call handling costs and elevated agent performance.

11

TIPS TO IMPORVE YOUR CUSTOMER SERVICE

Dealing with customers in today's business and commercial world is not just part of the job but something that large corporations, commercial industries and small businesses are basing their marketing strategies on. Corporations such as large hardware stores use "where you still get service" as their advertising slogan. Customers and clients today not only require but also expect good quality customer service. There is a well known saying in the business industry that you do something right and a customer will tell one person, but do something wrong and they will tell ten people. This is a good motto to use in any workplace.

The customer is always right and this well known phrase is still applicable in all situations, though plans need to be set in place to insure that both you and your customer benefit from the outcome and to insure that the right decisions are made by your staff. It is important for your staff when dealing with a disgruntled and angry client or customer to remain calm and listen carefully to what the customer is saying or trying to say. By listening to what the customer has to say your staff can understand what the problem is that the customer is experiencing and also what they intend for you to do to correct the problem.

Listening to your clients' problems enables you to be sympathetic and understanding, which will make your client feel that you care and provide them with a sense of security in a possibly hostile situation. When creating your Dealing with Customers Guideline it is important to make note of all the possible solutions and outcomes for that situation, by listening intently to your customer. Here are five quick tips for improving customer service.

— *Hire Good People*: When hiring customer service representatives make sure you recruit employees who will serve your customers well. Employees who are enthusiastic, friendly and outgoing will generally be nice to customers even in the most difficult situations. It's also important that new hires be intelligent, empathetic and have good problem solving skills. If they have those characteristics, they should have no problem understanding a situation and making the right decisions to keep the customer happy.

— *Invest in Customer Service Training Programmes*: Provide ongoing training that focuses on customer service. Customer service training should include role play scenarios of all types of customer interactions. For example, in the future, it's possible that a customer may swear at one of your employees and call them bad names. Role play the scenario with your employees and make sure they know how to handle these worst-case scenarios.

— *Empower Employees*: Nothing hurts customer service more than an unempowered employee. Give your employees the authority to make tough decisions on the fly, even if you are not around. Never second-guess their decisions. However, it's important to define customer service guidelines so they at least have a baseline from which to make their decisions. When an employee makes a good customer service decision, make sure to congratulate them on a job well done.

— *Get Customer Feedback*: Ask customers how you are doing. Customers are usually thrilled to have the opportunity to tell you what you are doing right and where there's room for improvement. Every so often, call up a customer at random and talk to them. You might also try using some of the web-based survey tools that are out there. It's easy to do market research and find out what your customers want. But don't forget to act on what you hear – you don't want to get a reputation for listening to customers but never acting on their feedback.

— *Surprise and Delight Customers*: Studies show that customers who are given exceptional customer service are better customers than those who are given just good customer service. They buy more and they stay on longer as customers. Every so often, surprise and delight your customers by doing something truly extraordinary.

IMPORTANCE OF CUSTOMER SERVICE ROLE PLAYS

Customer service role playing is a critical component of an effective customer service training programme. Here are some customer service role plays tips to get the most out of the exercise. It's hard to conceive of a customer service training programme that doesn't include at least some role-playing elements. But too often, customer service role plays come off as hokey and ineffective. Is it possible to keep role plays interesting? And what kinds of role plays are most useful for your customer service staff?

Customer service role plays are important because they give your employees opportunities to learn and make mistakes without consequences. In a real world scenario, a bungled call can quickly turn a current customer into a former customer. But in a role play, every call is a learning moment not just for the individuals participating in the role play, but for the entire staff.

As much as possible, you should try to set up scenarios that challenge your employees and cover the full range of customer requests. Although it might be tempting to try to cram every possible problem into a single "nightmare" call scenario, it's better to focus each scenario on one or two issues to maintain parallels to actual customer service calls. The scenarios you establish should include the following:

— Calls relating to product returns and exchanges.

— Problems with incomplete or wrong orders.

— Payment issues such as incorrect credit card charges and billing errors.

— Requests for information about specific products and product lines.

— Angry customers who are generally dissatisfied with the company and demand remedies for their complaints.

In this day and age, it might even be a good idea to establish role plays concerning emergency scenarios such as direct threats against the company, your stores, and individual employees.

CUSTOMER AND CUSTOMER SERVICE

The training session leader has the responsibility of assigning roles for both the customer and the customer service representative. At times, the leader may find it helpful to play the role of the customer herself. However, it is also useful to allow the customer service reps themselves play the role of the customer.

By pretending to be a customer, staff members gain a customer perspective and can more easily anticipate responses when they find themselves in a real world, customer service situation. A great way to keep everyone focused and attentive during role plays is to periodically switch new people into each role. If staff members know they may be asked to jump into the role play at any moment, they will be more likely to pay attention and remain engaged.

At the end of each role play, you should debrief your staff about what you learned. Start by asking the person who played the customer service provider how he thought the role play went. Then ask the "customer' and the rest of the group to give their perspectives about what worked and what didn't.

Finally, ask both the customer service provider and the rest of the group to talk about what they might do differently next time. It's also appropriate for you – the trainer – to interject your thoughts into the conversation, but only after staff members have had the opportunity to process the role play themselves.

CUSTOMER SERVICE IMPROVEMENT TRAINING

Need help with customer service improvement training sessions? If you are wondering how to improve customer service. When asked, most small business owners point to product quality as their company's biggest strength. But in business, product quality doesn't mean a thing if you don't have a high-quality customer service programme backing up your merchandise. If customer service is costing you business, maybe it's time for a little improvement training.

The simple truth is that a lot of customers base their purchasing decisions on service – not product quality. So from a competitive standpoint, the more effort you invest in improving your customer service programme, the more effective your business will be in capturing its share of the market. You could take a piecemeal approach to improving your customer service, but it's usually better to engage with an improvement training programme that is capable of improving the quality of service across the organisation.

Whenever possible, hire an outside consultant to lead improvement training sessions. Outsiders bring a fresh perspective to the situation and are more willing to embrace change because they have no investment in maintain the status quo. But regardless of whether or not you bring in an outsider, it's important for everyone in the organisation to be engaged in the process. With that in mind, here is what customer service improvement could look like for your business:

Session 1: Clarify Goals

Although it's up to you how long each training session lasts, it's not uncommon for each session to stretch out over a day or two.

In the first session, management and supervisors gather to address the company's customer service goals. One of the key issues to be discussed is the gap between actual customer service and the ideal level of service the company's leaders would like to provide.

Session 2: Frontline Customer Service Providers

Company leaders communicate their goals to the organisation's customer service providers and solicit their input. Even though it is management's responsibility to establish customer service goals, customer service providers need to feel invested in the process and should be able to express their thoughts on the subject in a collaborative training environment.

Session 3: Develop an Implementation Plan

The implementation session involves both company leaders and frontline service providers. At this stage in the process, you have presumably established where you want to go with customer service. This session focuses on how the organisation will go about getting there.

Everyone's input is welcome, but by the end of this session company leaders and service providers should have a written implementation plan clearly describing the role each person will play in improving the organisation's ability to meet its customers needs. If additional training is required, management should identify training opportunities and communicate their expectations for participation.

Sessions 4: Conduct Follow-Up

Follow-up sessions are possibly the most critical sessions in the entire process. They can involve management only sessions as well as sessions for everyone in the organisation. When you schedule these sessions is up to you. The important thing is that you use them to evaluate your progress and make adjustments as needed.

BAD CUSTOMER SERVICE

Bad customer service examples offer great lessons on how to improve customer service. These customer service horror stories will give you a laugh and a lesson. Real-world examples are a great tool for training your customer service staff.

Some of the best examples are negative examples – case studies of what not to do in response to a customer request or complaint. To help get the ball rolling, we've provided several examples of actual customer service scenarios, reported by customers themselves.

GOOD CUSTOMER SERVICE EMPLOYEES

Recruiting good customer service employees is the first step to take in any customer service improvement initiative. Fire the bad CSRs and start over. You don't have to play with the hand you've been dealt. Customer service is your lifeline to the people who purchase your products and services.

So then why would you entrust your customer service functions to people who are unqualified and uninterested in treating your customers right? Good customer service begins with hiring. Here's the information you need to recruit the best candidates for the job.

According to some estimates, up to 60% of small businesses have the wrong people working in their customer service departments. Although the reasons for this are complex, much of the blame rests on the business owners themselves.

While other positions may require specialised knowledge and experience, it's generally assumed that almost anyone is capable of fielding calls from customers. In reality, effective customer service requires a unique blend of personality and a skill set designed to meet the specific needs of that business' customers.

Personality Requirements

Right out of the gate, you need to look for individuals who are outgoing, but not "chatty"; assertive, but not abrasive; and responsive, but not a pushover. This definition alone eliminates a significant percentage of the people who are already working in the customer service field. Don't assume that prior customer service experience translates into a personality compatible with the field. Get to know them and make your own judgement.

Technology Requirements

One of the ironies of customer service is that employers often spend tons of cash on sophisticated call centre technology and then hire the least qualified, minimum wage workers they can find to operate it. Hiring individuals who aren't qualified to man your call center technology is a recipe for disaster. At the very least, customer service candidates need to be familiar with modern office technology and demonstrate a willingness to be trained in the specific call center technology your business relies on.

Industry Requirements

A business uses vocabulary and processes that are specific to its industry. Front line customer service personnel have to be conversant in the industry in order to successfully respond to customer concerns. They don't have to be experts, but it definitely helps if candidates have either prior experience or some other connection to your industry.

In some cases, a qualified candidate may be given a crash course in industry jargon and receive ongoing exposure to the industry through additional training venues.

Employee Retention

The best thing you can do to make sure the right personnel are staffing your customer service department is to retain the people who are doing the job effectively right now.

The combined value of a quality customer service rep's knowledge and experience are not easily replaceable. Aside from the learning curve associated with bringing a new worker up to speed, the financial costs of successfully hiring a replacement can be substantial. It's much easier to invest in current customer service personnel with respectable salaries and career development resources.

CUSTOMER SERVICE PERFORMANCE

Customer service performance reviews are the linchpin tactic that allows you to improve customer service. Without feedback on performance, customer service reps will never improve. Your company policy requires annual performance reviews of every person you employ. Unfortunately, it doesn't tell you how to do them.

Other workers can be reviewed on the basis of sales volume or production data, but how do you review your customer service personnel?

Although it is slightly more challenging to give substantive performance reviews of customer service employees, it can be done. As much as possible, the key is to establish objective measurements of the employees' abilities to achieve their goals and meet your expectations as an employer.

The ideal scenario is to incorporate performance criteria into a single form that can be tailored to specifically evaluate customer service workers. Even though the performance criteria for customer service personnel is different than the criteria for workers in other departments, all customer service employees must be judged according to the same criteria to limit the company's legal liability.

Knowledge and Skills

An employee's ability to do their job is limited by their knowledge of your company's customer service processes and functions. A solid performance review measures the worker's understanding of the company's specific customer service procedures. But it also measures the worker's broader customer service skills in the areas of phone etiquette, interpersonal communication, and customer relationships.

Another important factor is the employee's mastery of the software and call center technology required to successfully fulfil their responsibilities.

Additionally, customer service staff should be evaluated on the quality of their work. Does the individual promptly respond to customer needs? Do they complete follow-up tasks in a timely manner? It's difficult to answer these questions on your own, especially if you aren't the employee's immediate supervisor. Don't hesitate to solicit input from others in the organisation *before* you meet with the employee face-to-face.

Attitude counts—particularly when the employee works in a customer service capacity. All customer service personnel should be expected to maintain a friendly, yet professional demeanour with both customers and co-workers. You may find it helpful to implement call monitoring technology to randomly assess the employee's attitude throughout the year.

Excessive absenteeism is a drag on productivity and employee morale. Similarly, extended break periods and tardiness can be a sign that an employee is not as committed as they should be. Publish attendance requirements in the employee handbook and incorporate attendance into the discussion during the performance review. Although specific attendance problems should be addressed as they occur, the annual review gives you the opportunity to identify root problems and discuss alternatives with the employee.

Finally, a performance review should evaluate the employee's adherence to company policies and procedures. Any problems with authority should be highlighted and consequences of further noncompliance should be clearly communicated during the course of the review process.

NON-PROFIT ORGANISATIONS

Customer service in non-profit organisations? You bet! Customer service is a universal challenge and a universal opportunity. The term "customer service" usually brings to mind a call centre fielding customer complaints for a mass retailer or service provider. But customer service is playing an increasingly important role in a wide range of organisations, including nonprofits. The challenging part is trying to adapt traditional customer service programmes for use in an environment where profit isn't the most important goal.

If you expect nonprofit customer service techniques to look similar to customer service techniques in a for-profit venture, you're right. In a lot of ways, the two are virtually indistinguishable. Employees are trained to provide friendly, courteous service to the organisation's base.

The difference lies in the fact that a nonprofit's base is a little more complex than a business' base. While for-profit customer service interfaces primarily with customers, nonprofit customer service interfaces with three different categories of people: Donors, volunteers, and programme participants.

A nonprofit's customer service to donors involves establishing and maintaining relationships with existing donors, as well as individuals who exhibit potential to become donors in the near future. In theory, everyone the organisation comes into contact with is a potential donor.

However, customer service personnel and front line staff need to be trained to identify "hot prospects", and equipped to help them take the next step. Since information is critical for donors, donor customer service largely amounts to creating opportunities to inform donors without appearing pushy or manipulative.

Volunteers are another important—but often overlooked—category of people in a nonprofit. Many nonprofits would be unable to survive without the sacrificial efforts of their volunteer base. Unfortunately, nonprofit volunteers are sometimes treated like unpaid employees, with little recognition of their vital contribution to the organisation.

Effective nonprofit customer service goes the extra mile to recognise volunteers and to facilitate the achievement of their individual goals. Everyone from the CEO to the receptionist should be taught to engage volunteers in conversations that encourage a mutual exchange of ideas.

12

DEVELOPING EFFECTIVE CUSTOMER SERVICE CULTURE

Customer service is not merely customer relations or how nice frontline workers are to customers. Rather, satisfying or even delighting customers is the goal of excellent customer service. Because customers for different types of services have different needs, customer service strategies will differ and must be tailored to the target customer.

It improves trust and information exchange. In the public sector, including child support offices, good customer service generates satisfied or delighted customers. Satisfied customers lead to increased compliance, improved information exchange, improved relationships, increased trust, and, potentially, decreased workloads or costs. For instance, police departments across the country have embraced the concept of community policing.

Through community policing, police departments incorporate a customer focus as well as an attitude of partnership with customers, to increase satisfaction and trust and even reduce fear of crime in the community. Customers actually participate in addressing crime and disorder problems, thus reducing the workload on patrol officers.

It saves money and increases profit. In the private sector, good customer service leads to satisfied or delighted customers, which generates customer loyalty, which produces increased revenues and reduced costs.

The public and private sector customer service literature concurs on the process for delivering great customer service, even if outcomes differ. In the private sector, profit and growth are the outcomes, not goals. Profit and growth are generated by customer loyalty. Loyalty is generated by customer satisfaction.

Customer satisfaction is the goal that companies should seek and focus on, because high customer satisfaction, as a matter of course, produces customer loyalty and subsequently profit and growth. At this point, the public and private sectors converge—customer satisfaction is the goal.

Customer satisfaction is achieved by providing valued services and products, where value is the positive difference between customers' actual experiences and their service delivery expectations. Productive employees also create value. Employee productivity stems from employee loyalty, and loyalty is a product of employee satisfaction. Satisfaction is generated by high-quality support services and by being empowered to provide value and resolve customer complaints.

This customer service culture must be supported by leadership that emphasizes the importance of each customer and employee. These leaders must be creative and energetic, participatory and caring (not removed or elitist), that is, one who can be a coach, teacher, or listener (not just a supervisor or manager). Such a leader demonstrates company values (rather than simply institutionalising policies) and motivates by mission.

In the customer service literature, five guiding principles are adopted by public as well as private agencies delivering excellent customer service:

1. Embrace change and persistently strive to improve.
2. Continually ask the target customers what they want and then give it to them.
3. Empower, support, and reward frontline personnel.
4. Harness the power of information.
5. Establish an enabling infrastructure.

DEVELOPING CUSTOMER SERVICE CULTURE

Begin by identifying the target customers and by considering the point of purchase, point of service delivery or receipt, and point of consumption. Cluster or segment target customers based on their common behaviours, knowing that targeting the wrong customers can have adverse effects on the organisation. Determine the priorities of various clusters of customers, knowing that the capabilities of the organisation are crucial in addressing these priorities.

When possible, focus on customers with high current or future value. This does not mean that other customers will not receive service, but it may mean that they will receive a different level of service. Consider the frequent flier programmes that airlines and hotels offer to their customers with high current and future value. This does not mean that other passengers will not receive services, but services may not be at the same level.

Discourage non-target customers, those who are not likely to be satisfied by the services, and those to whom it is expensive to provide services, which is a necessary part of a customer focus.

Determine what target customers want (not just what they need right now) by asking them in person or as part of a mail or telephone survey or by using other mechanisms (e.g., electronic tracking and researching marketing trends) to determine what they want. Be aware that advertising, word of mouth, and public relations influence customers' expectations. Meeting customers' basic needs or expectations does not always bring high levels of satisfaction. Exceeding expectations produces high satisfaction—therefore, determine customers' ideal desires.

Determine how the target customers prioritise their "wants." Generally, customers want convenience, quality products and services, variety or selection, low prices, and protection or security. However, each organisation must identify what is most important to its customers. Weigh how important the customer-identified "wants" are to the organisation. Are the services something that the organisation does, is capable of doing, or wants to pursue?

Determine how well the organisation can meet the customers' "wants" in comparison with competitors. The success of other companies at meeting and exceeding customer expectations changes a customer's frame of reference and increases a customer's expectations. Determine which "wants," if performance delivery were to be improved, would most impact the organisation's bottom line.

Influence of Organisational Culture

Utilising the information gathered, establish the company's customer-focused vision. The vision statement should be simple and may also identify what the company does not want to be.

Live up to what is promised by concurrently developing and applying externally and internally oriented strategic service concepts that reflect the vision. If the organisation does not implement both internally and externally oriented service strategies consistent with the vision, the organisation will have good intentions but poor customer service. Continually reflect on the vision and goals and the way services are delivered to customers. Be creative about the mechanisms used to create and deliver new services. Be willing to change existing practices to integrate improvements.

Externally Oriented Strategic Service

The externally oriented strategic service concept establishes how the organisation's service is designed, marketed, and delivered to target customers. Take into account the costs of providing services and ways to minimise those costs while implementing quality control.

The service concept must be developed with the frontline worker at its center. Determine the necessary financial, human, and technological resources necessary, as well as how the organisational structure and flow can enable the frontline worker to delight the customer and deliver the promised vision.

Use advertising/educational strategies to set appropriate customer expectations. When planning, realise that control of information can take the place of assets. Provide a feedback loop for incorporating customer comments and complaints into the planning processes.

Customer complaints are an invaluable resource and source of information without which organisations cannot be successful. Complaints brought to the organisation are one of the most efficient and least expensive ways to obtain information about customer expectations of products and services.

Another means of soliciting customer feedback that has been implemented by a number of service leaders is to interview lost customers—those who have switched service providers. Still other options are holding customer meetings, hosting social events, and attending seminars or conferences where customers are present.

Internally Oriented Strategic Service

The internally oriented strategic service concept establishes how the organisation's internal processes will support the customer-focused vision. The premise behind the internally oriented strategic service concept is capable workers who are well trained and fairly compensated provide better service, need less supervision, and are much more likely to stay on the job.

Ensure that leaders of the learning organisation exhibit the company values. Leaders must foster the creation and testing of new ideas and be unabashedly willing to change existing practices to integrate improvements. Identify employee groups important to implementing the externally oriented service concept. Frontline workers are of central importance.

Identify the characteristics and needs of the employee group(s) and how well those needs are met. This may include resources needed to successfully perform the job or needs can refer to compensation, work environmental factors, or personal needs.

Understanding employee needs helps an organisation to develop successful processes as well as employee retention policies. Learn how targeted employees perceive the proposed customer services. An organisation cannot change without the participation of its employees.

Focus on recruiting employees who support the customer service vision. The costs of employing people who do not support the customer service vision are considerable. Empower frontline employees to do what it takes to satisfy the customer. Management must support employee empowerment by clearly defining the parameters of the empowerment, while remaining flexible within the parameters. This will encourage creativity.

Ensure that management supports employee decisions and judgement calls, even if this means that the cost of satisfying customers initially increases.

In positions of high customer contact, quality control is not met by increased supervision, but by the use of incentives to emphasise quality, making service providers highly visible to customers, and by building a peer group to instill a sense of pride and teamwork.

Ensure that divisions and individuals within the organisation communicate. Frontline employees and other employees need information and a support network. A customer should never have to tell one employee what another employee already knows.

Develop cross-functional teams for operations and improvement tasks. First ask those who are doing the work for suggestions to improve productivity.

If you look at companies lauded for their superior customer service, you almost always find that those companies create a culture that supports excellence in customer service. It's not that they simply train their employees in customer service skills. What they do is ensure that customer service is interwoven into everything the company does. Customer service excellence simply becomes the way things are done around here.

In fact, the way things are done around here is a good, simple description of organisational culture. With respect to customer service, a customer service culture involves a set of beliefs, values, and action options that are communicated to all members of the organisation, so they can be used to guide and mold interactions and decision-making regarding customers.

The best way to understand this is to look at two companies in the retaill industry, one with a culture that supports excellence in customer service, and another where the company's culture is oriented towards immediate or short term monetary gain.

Company A interweaves the idea of providing excellent customer service in everything they do. Their sales staff are not paid on commission, but paid a basic salary, and the staff is taught (via training, coaching, and observing management behaviour), that it's more important to keep a customer (and keep a customer happy), than to make a one time sale.

Company B, however, is much more concerned with making the sale. Their staff are paid on a commission basis, and employees are encouraged to spend their time selling to new customers, rather than interacting with existing customers. Any activity that is not directly related to increasing short term sales is frowned upon.

Most of us are familiar with such companies. Go to Company A (that has a customer service oriented culture), and you'll get questions answered before and after the sale, not be pressured to commit to a sale, and a focus on providing you with good information at all times.

Go to Company B, however, and you'll find staff disinterested in you if you indicate you are just looking, a hesitancy to spend time answering questions, and much less effective post-sale customer service. Most of us will patronise Company B, even if their prices are a little higher, because they convey a send of trustworthiness. We like to go to Company A, and we don't enjoy going to Company B. The upshot is that Company A has made a concerted effort to create a customer service oriented culture, while Company B has created a culture that supports making money through new sales.

CREATING A CUSTOMER SERVICE CULTURE

In the dynamic world of retail, companies often talk about the importance of customer service excellence and the dramatic effect that it can have on the profitability of a business. The fast paced, competitive retail environment is a constant challenge for retail owners. It is easy to become reactive rather than maintain a proactive approach that will lead them towards their company's vision.

Retailers understand the importance of delivering Superior Customer Service that exceeds their competitors. How can retailers ensure that their people strive for a high level of service? Here are 6 simple tips:

1. *Recruit the right people:* The recruitment process is crucial in developing strong customer focused teams. Employers must ensure that the interview process effectively determines the suitability of potential employees. Behavioural questions will help assess whether the person will suit a retail environment together with the culture fit of the company.
2. *Train rain your people:* The Induction process together with the ongoing training of your people is imperative to your staff's future success. Customer Service must be a strong focus in the training process. New employees must receive a job description that clearly outlines the expectations of the role. This will ensure that the employee feels confident and will reach their full potential.
3. *Minimise tasks:* Tasks are part of any job but a business with strong customer focus understands the importance of keeping those tasks to a minimum. Companies must be mindful of all tasks effecting the business, like those silent e-mails from different departments that involve extra tasks.

Visual merchandising is also a great tool to enhance product and make sales but don't make it too much of a focus and take your staff away from the most important person, the customer.

4. *Effective staffing levels:* When sales are down, one of the first places targeted for change is in the reduction of staffing levels. This is an important cost factor but be mindful of analysing each business carefully. Don't underestimate the potential and needs of your business or your people.
5. *Walk the Talk:* A customer service culture begins at the top. All actions and words must reflect this vision from everyone in the company. From policy & procedure manuals, Induction programmes, memos from Head office and executive store visits. All of the above must reflect the Customer First vision at all times.
6. *Reward on Service:* Recognise the performance of your staff's customer service ability. Set goals based on exceeding customer's expectations and reward your staff on achieving them. This will build confidence, increase staff morale and help promote healthy competition within your team.

Changing Customer Service Culture

Speculation as to the reasons why customer service is at the low level it is today is rampant. The reasons are numerous—more sophisticated customers, a generational change of employee attitudes toward work, more outsourcing of customer service call centers overseas, and too much technology are just a few. Each of these things contributes to the current levels.

The problem is much more deeply rooted. Too many companies think there is a quick fix for their customer service problems, as opposed to making a long-term commitment to quality that is accepted by everyone in the organisation, top to bottom.

The fact that the quick-fix solutions will not work, what methods of implementing change can be utilised that will indeed result in cultural changes in a company? What are some of the things an organisation can do to cause a lasting change in its customer service performance? Here are some simple ideas that can produce profound results:

1. Have real expectations of the results of seminars and speakers. These programmes should be used to introduce new ideas or to support existing programmes but never to be used in lieu of other processes. There is no magic potion for service. It has to be ongoing and an inherent part of the culture of the organisation. Seminars and speakers are effective catalysts of service culture, but they are never to be confused with the solution. The solution is the relentless pursuit of service combined with values.

2. Make sure the top-line executives of the organisation know that customer service is serious business to the company. It cannot be lip service; senior management must take service very seriously. Remember that employees observe management and how it supports this culture. They will act accordingly.

3. Keep the key issues of the company's service beliefs and principles alive via regular meetings and discussions. The basic service principles of the organisation should be mentioned at every meeting in the organisation. There should be no exceptions to this. Discussions of the quest for service should be second-nature when meetings occur. Employees

should be sincerely commended when they report that they have done something for a customer.

4. Make sure that written correspondence—from internal memos to email correspondence—includes references to service. Every e-mail that is sent, therefore, makes a stated commitment to service. This creates an atmosphere of "lifting the bar" that causes the employees to be consistently aware that they have stated the importance of service and they must live up to their commitment.
5. Emphasise the beliefs and principles with new employees. New employees should have no question regarding the importance of service in the organisation. The focus on customer service should be reinforced during any orientation as well as the natural mentoring that will take place with new hires. From interviews, to welcome sessions, to training, through indoctrination, service must be stressed.
6. Make sure that your company Website communicates the passion for service that exists in the organisation. Websites are more and more becoming the front door for businesses. A Website is an extension of the company to prospects and customers in the same way that the receptionist or operator is the front door to your company.
7. Make sure that executives and managers are interacting with customers. Senior managers too often operate with the concept that they have "paid their dues" and that they don't need to interact with customers any more. They feel they have reached a level that is above spending time with customers and would rather dictate to others in the organisation what their customers are thinking and how to deal with them!

8. Treat your customer service reps as importantly as you treat your sales reps. If you've ever noticed the lavish awards, banquets, and recognition that most companies heap on their sales representatives, you've probably also noticed the absence of recognition of the customer service contact people. Companies have migrated toward a fairly common belief that the name of the business game is new sales while often losing sight of the fact that it takes more cost to acquire a new customer than it does to maintain an existing one.

CUSTOMER SATISFACTION

Customer satisfaction, a business term, is a measure of how products and services supplied by a company meet or surpass customer expectation. It is seen as a key performance indicator within business and is part of the four perspectives of a Balanced Scorecard.

In a competitive marketplace where businesses compete for customers, customer satisfaction is seen as a key differentiator and increasingly has become a key element of business strategy.

Organisations are increasingly interested in retaining existing customers while targeting non-customers; measuring customer satisfaction provides an indication of how successful the organisation is at providing products and/or services to the marketplace.

Customer satisfaction is an ambiguous and abstract concept and the actual manifestation of the state of satisfaction will vary from person to person and product/service to product/service.

The state of satisfaction depends on a number of both psychological and physical variables which correlate with satisfaction behaviours such as return and recommend rate. The level of satisfaction can also vary depending on other options the customer may have and other products against which the customer can compare the organisation's products.

Because satisfaction is basically a psychological state, care should be taken in the effort of quantitative measurement, although a large quantity of research in this area has recently been developed.

Work done by Berry, Brodeur between 1990 and 1998 defined ten 'Quality Values' which influence satisfaction behaviour, further expanded by Berry in 2002 and known as the ten domains of satisfaction. These ten domains of satisfaction include: Quality, Value, Timeliness, Efficiency, Ease of Access, Environment, Interdepartmental Teamwork, Front line Service Behaviours, Commitment to the Customer and Innovation.

These factors are emphasised for continuous improvement and organisational change measurement and are most often utilised to develop the architecture for satisfaction measurement as an integrated model.

Work done by Parasuraman, Zeithaml and Berry between 1985 and 1988 provides the basis for the measurement of customer satisfaction with a service by using the gap between the customer's expectation of performance and their perceived experience of performance. This provides the measurer with a satisfaction "gap" which is objective and quantitative in nature.

Work done by Cronin and Taylor propose the "confirmation/disconfirmation" theory of combining the "gap" described by Parasuraman, Zeithaml and Berry as two different measures into a single measurement of performance according to expectation. According to Garbrand, customer satisfaction equals perception of performance divided by expectation of performance.

Customer Satisfaction Keys

As markets become more sophisticated and customers more demanding, competition between business is becoming stiffer. Whether it's the corner service station, Bill's Plumbing Service, an environmental consulting firm or an industrial cleaning service, competition is fierce.

In today's economy, the customer is king, and most have adopted the attitude of "If I or my company choose to spend money with you, you have to earn it." The result is that in virtually every industry, a multitude of businesses offering similar products and services are now zealously competing on price, quality, quantity and just about anything else they can offer.

So what differentiates one organisation from another? How does a company attract customers? More importantly, how does it hold onto them? Ultimately, there is one major area in which a business can distinguish itself, offer added value and gain a competitive edge—superior customer service.

Customer service pays. It does not cost. But it does mean everyone in the organisation has to get involved. Whatever the size or nature of your business, whatever your role in the company, you're involved in customer service. How you react then, will have an effect on everything your company is trying to achieve because everyone is an ambassador for the organisation.

The management guru, Peter Drucker states, "The purpose of a business is to create and retain customers." So where do you start? Following are seven customer service tips that can help ensure your organisation is, indeed, providing superior customer service that will pretty much guarantee a high retention rate.

1. *Know Your Customer*: Understand what it is about your organisation that makes customers come to

you instead of your competition. Identify your strengths and build upon them.

2. *Know Your Competition*: Know what your competition is doing at all times. Are they doing something new or different? Are they doing something better than you? How can you do something better than them? Always ask yourself these questions. Keep your business on top when it comes to quality of products and service.
3. *Retain Your Customers*: It can cost 5-10 times more to acquire a new customer than it does to keep an existing one. Keep your customers delighted. Treat them like gold. After all, the customers are the reason we are in business. And remember, every customer you lose is a customer gained by your competition!
4. *Create a Positive First Impression*: The first contact your customers have with your organisation is critical. Take measures to make sure that first contact is a magic moment instead of a tragic moment. In these days of shrinking profit margins, little things can make a big difference. Mother Theresa put it very well when she said, "Kind words can be short and easy to speak, but their echoes are truly endless."
5. *Approach Complaints with a Positive Attitude*: When you're dealing with customers on an ongoing basis, you'll undoubtedly receive your fair share of complaints. So keep in mind: "Don't take it personally, it's just business." After that, it's simply a question of approaching the problem with the right attitude to ensure customer satisfaction.
6. *Sharpen Your Customer Service Skills*: Customer service training is the most valuable tool you can give yourself or, as a manager, your employees.

The skills mastered will enable everyone to become more productive, enjoy their job more, increase their value to the company and improve customer service at all levels.

7. *Measure Customer Satisfaction.* Continuously monitor your business. Never sit back and relax. Offer new products or services as needs require. Always ask the customer what you can do better. That information is the vital link between your business and your customers and can help provide the kind of service and satisfaction that builds customers for life.

In any business today, the superior customer service commitment must be renewed every day. We have to tend to it, we have to feed it, we have to care about it and we have to live it. When we do, that commitment translates into delighted customers, repeat business, referrals and increased profits.

ACHIEVE EXCELLENCE CUSTOMER SERVICE

Customers have developed a great deal in recent years as they have become more aware of business practises, demand a high level of service and have more companies to choose who to buy from. This has led many organisations to separate themselves from their competition through excellent customer service, instead of using traditional methods, such as product development or diversification.

This makes perfect business sense as research has shown that it costs 6 times more to recruit a new customer compared with maintaining and building relationships with current customers. Whether an organisation is a huge internationally known corporation or a small company that operates in a niche market, the customer service that they both provide is key to their success.

This is because a strong customer service strategy generates many benefits such as:

— Enables strong relationships to be built,

— Easier to gain repeat business,

— Saves resources through maximising,

— Opportunities with current clients,

— Improves an organisations image,

— Creates positive word-of-mouth,

— Opens doors with other organisations through recommendations.

— Adds value to a product or service.

— Excellent customer service is hard to copy and be maintained by competitors.

For an organisation to truly benefit from customer service the policies and attitudes need to exist throughout the whole organisation; in effect they need to be lived and breathed everyday and in every situation. Due to the importance of gaining a consistent approach, many organisations invest in customer service training heavily.

Customer service training initiatives are one of the most popular training areas in business. This strengthens how important organisations view customer service to be. Many topics exist under customer service, such as telephone skills, face-to-face, complaints handling, etc. all of which are important areas. Different learning and development specialists have different approaches on how best to address each topic.

The best methods and topics depend on the external providers expertise, experience, and the organisations problem that they are tackling. Learning and development specialists are there to help organisations develop their employees, be it in leadership, equality and diversity, management, etc. Righttrack Consultancy has a vast experience in many training areas, including customer service.

One of their specialisms is working with organisations to create unique development programmes that make a real difference. They say the key to generating a strong customer focus approach in an organisation is to work together to change the perceptions and behaviour of employees.

A vital element to the success of a customer service training programme is getting employees to buy into the programme. A great way to do this is to make the programme fun and engaging and stay away from lecture based programmes as these hinder interaction.

Elements of a development programme that encourages interaction include experiential events, role-plays, and the use of actors, all of which encourage discussion in a fun way.

Customer service is an interesting training subject and many organisations can benefit from sprucing up their current offering. This does not need to be a daunting experience, as learning and development specialists are there to use their expertise to help create a training programme that fulfils an organisations needs.

Achieve Excellence in Sales

For an organisation to truly benefit from customer service the policies and attitudes need to exist throughout the whole organisation; in effect they need to be lived and breathed everyday and in every situation. Most people are striving to better themselves. It's only natural. People are seeking better lives for themselves and for their families. Most want to improve their standard of living, increase their income, and put aside some money for a rainy day. Check the sales figures on the number of self-improvement books sold each year. It is an indication of people's awareness that in order to better themselves, they must continue improving their abilities.

To excel in any selling situation, you must have confidence. Confidence comes first and foremost from knowledge. You have to understand yourself and your goals in order to develop an attitude of self-confidence. You must identify and accept your weaknesses as well as your special talents. This requires a personal honesty that not everyone is capable of exercising.

In any sales effort, you must accept other people as they are, not as you would wish them to be. One of the most common faults among sales people is impatience. When the prospective customer is slow to understand or make a decision, too often a salesman becomes aggravated or overlay aggressive.

The successful salesperson handles these situations the same as he would if he were asking a girl for a date, or even applying for a new job. He takes his time. He listens closely to the other person. He directs the conversation toward positive aspects rather than negative ones.

Knowing your product, making a clear sales presentation to qualified prospects, and closing more sales will take a lot less time once you know your own capabilities and failings, and come to understand and care about the prospects upon whom you are calling.

Because our society is built upon commerce, all of us are selling something all the time. Even if we are not promoting a specific product, we are least selling an image of ourselves to those around us. We are projecting personalities that we hope others will accept and to which they will respond favourably. We move up or stand still in direct relation to the sales efforts.

Everyone is included, whether we're attempting to be a friend to a co-worker, a neighbour, or selling big real estate projects. Accepting these facts will enable you to understand that there is no such thing as a born salesman. Indeed, in selling, we all begin at the same starting line, and we all have the same finish line as the goal a successful sale.

Recognising that we're all sales people in one way or another whether we're attempting to move up from forklift driver to warehouse manager, waitress to hostess, salesman to sales manager, or from mail order dealer to president of the largest sales organisation in the world it's vitally important that we continue learning. Only by applying ourselves to the never-ending task of self-improvement will we ever be able to cross that line from mediocrity to success.

Utilising the proper tools, anyone can sell virtually anything to virtually anybody. While it is true that there are some items that are easier to sell than others, and while some people work harder at selling than others, regardless of what you're promoting or even how you're attempting to do it, the odds can be in your favour. If you make your presentation to enough people, you'll find a buyer.

The problem with most people is in making contact and getting their sales presentation seen, read, or heard by enough prospects. But this really shouldn't be a problem. The principle error is one of impatience. With training this impatience can be harnessed to work in the salesperson's favour.

Getting up out of bed in the morning and doing what has to be done in order to sell more units of your product keeping records, updating your materials, planning the direction of further sales efforts, and all the while increasing your own knowledge requires a great deal of personal motivation, discipline, and energy. But the rewards can be beyond your wildest dreams. Make no mistake about it, the selling profession is the highest paid occupation in the world!

Selling is challenging. It demands the utmost of your creativity and innovative thinking. The greater your desire to succeed and the deeper your dedication toward the achievement of your goals, the more you'll sell. Thousands of people the world over become millionaires each year through selling. Many of them were flat broke and unable to find a regular job when they began their selling careers. Yet, they've created success. You can do it too!

Selling is the best way to achieve wealth. You get paid according to your own efforts, skill, and knowledge of people. If you're ready to become rich, then seriously consider selling a product or service preferably something exclusively yours that you have created yourself. Choose something that you write, manufacture, or produce for the benefit of other people. Outside of this, the want ads are full of opportunities for ambitious sales people. You can start there, study, learn from experience, and watch for the chances that will allow you to move ahead by leaps and bounds.

Here are some basic guidelines that will allow you to increase your total sales and income. Like to call these tips the Commandments of Strategic Salesmanship. Look them over. Dedicate some thought to each suggestion. Adapt those that you can to your own selling efforts. You will likely be rewarded many times over for the brief investment of time you spend in studying these suggestions.

1. If the product you're selling is something your prospect can hold in his hands, get it into his hands as quickly as possible. Include the prospect in the presentation. Let him hold the product in his hand, feel it, weigh it, admire it.

2. Don't stand or sit alongside your prospect. Instead, face him while you're pointing out the important advantages of your product. This will enable you to watch his facial expressions and determine how and when you should begin to close the sale.
3. While handling sales literature, hold it by the top of the page, at the proper angle, so that your prospect can read it as you highlight the important points. You don't want to cover the text or any graphic elements in your sales literature that might help convince the client of the product's value. Also, don't release your hold on it. You want to be able to control the specific parts you want the prospect to read.
4. When you encounter a prospect who won't talk with you or provide feedback to your sales presentation, you must dramatise your presentation to get him involved. Stop and ask questions such as, "Now, don't you agree that this product can help you or would be of benefit to you?" After you've asked a question such as this, stop talking and wait for the prospect to answer. In most cases, following such a question, the one who talks first will lose. Don't say anything until after the prospect has given you some kind of answer. Wait him out!
5. Prospects who are themselves sales people or who imagine they know a lot about selling sometimes present difficult selling obstacles, especially for the novice. However, these prospects can be the easiest of all to sell. Give your sales presentation. Instead of trying for a close, toss out a challenge such as, "I don't know, Mr. Prospect. After watching your reactions to what I've been showing and telling you about my product, I'm very doubtful if this product can truthfully be of benefit to you." Then spend a

few seconds just looking at him and waiting for him to say something. Then, start packing up your sales materials as if you are about to leave. In almost every instance, your tough nut will quickly ask you, "Why?" These people are generally so filled with their own importance that they simply have to prove you wrong. When they start on this tangent, they will sell themselves. The more skeptical you are concerning their ability to make your product work to their benefit, the more they'll demand that you sell it to them. If you find that this prospect will not rise to your challenge, then go ahead with the packing of your sales materials and leave quickly. Some people are so self-centered that it is a poor use of your valuable time to attempt to convince them.

6. Remember that in selling, time is money! You must allocate only so much time to each prospect. The prospect who asks you to call back next week, or who wants to ramble on about similar products, prices, or previous experiences, is costing you money. Learn quickly to get the prospect interested in and wanting your product. Then systematically present your sales pitch through to the close when he signs on the dotted line and reaches for his checkbook. You must spend as much time as possible calling on new prospects. After the introductory call on your prospect, you should be selling products and collecting money. Any callbacks should be only for reorders, or to sell related products from your line. In other words, you can waste an introductory call on a prospect to qualify him, but you're going to be wasting money if you continue calling on him to sell him the first unit of your product. When faced with a reply such as, "Your product looks pretty good, but I'll have to

give it some thought," you should quickly jump in with a response. Ask him what it is that he doesn't understand, or what specifically about your product does he feel he needs to give more thought. Let him explain, and then go back into your sales presentation and make everything crystal clear for him. If he still balks, then you can either tell him that you think he's procrastinating, or that on the whole you don't think the product will really benefit him or that it's purchase will be to his advantage.

6. Review your sales presentation, your sales materials, and your prospecting efforts. Make sure you have a "door-opener" introduction that arouses interest and compels a purchase the first time around. This can be as simple as giving the customer a free item as an interest stimulator to make him more inclined to view your entire line. Offer a special marked-down price on an item that everybody wants. The important thing is to get the prospect on your list of current buyers and off your list of potential clients. After you have captured the first sale, follow up via mail or telephone with the related but more profitable products you have to offer.

Excellent Customer Service Tips

In the business world, good customer service often isn't good enough anymore. Customers and clients are becoming increasingly disenchanted with the merely adequate. For them, extraordinary service is the rule, not the exception. Anything less, and they're happy to vote with their feet and their wallets. That makes extraordinary service necessary, not just desirable. And that, in turn, mandates a strategy to help ensure that your business matches that standout service standard on a daily basis. Here are seven ideas and tips to help your business establish and maintain an ongoing climate of service excellence.

1. Define what extraordinary really means. It's an easy term to toss about, but knowing what exceptional service entails is essential to establishing the procedures and the mindset with which to achieve it. So, delineate what extraordinary means — is it lower price? Keeping appointments on time or making certain that telephone service reps always say "please" and "thank you"? By knowing precisely what is merely good enough — and what takes your business beyond that — you get a firm handle on what you need to do to hit that goal on a consistent basis.
2. Ask if you're not sure. Many companies may find it understandably difficult to genuinely pinpoint what extraordinary service really entails. So, do some legwork. Conduct focus groups with customers to see what they really value. Ask your complaint department, if you have one, to identify topics that are frequent targets of dissatisfaction. Often, you may find extraordinary translates to a holistic grouping of issues, not just one product or service. "Often, being extraordinary means offering someone a truly exceptional experience," says Dr. Noelle Nelson, author of *"The Power of Appreciation in Business."* "The quality of something may be good, but it's the overall experience that will really define customer loyalty."
3. Allow your people to be extraordinary. Saying you want extraordinary service and actually carrying it out is a tough nut without the necessary authority. One of the biggest challenges of providing a consistently top-drawer performance is shifting

conditions — what's appropriate for one customer may not work with another.. For instance, one customer may be so dissatisfied that a partial refund may be in order. By contrast, other customers who are a bit less peeved may be happy with a problem solved without any sort of refund. So, allow employees reasonable freedom of choice to read a situation and react accordingly. For instance, Nelson suggests giving employees a budgetary allotment which they can use, as needed, to address refunds or other unexpected costs associated with giving customers the benefit of the doubt. To illustrate: Southwest Airlines gives its telephone customer service reps the authority to OK refunds if a caller claims they didn't get the airfare they wanted.

4. Share information. If you run a retail business, business management tools, such as Microsoft's Retail Management System, can be invaluable in tracking critical data, such as what items and services are selling particularly well. If you have that data, don't keep it a state secret. Sharing the information with your employees lets them know what's hitting on all cylinders. It also helps them promote these products or services to customers. "Sharing information with others is a really positive step," says Nelson. In other words, don't keep critical customer information close to the vest. That holds true with businesses other than retail. For instance, Microsoft Dynamics Customer Relationship Management (CRM) software lets you share valuable information about clients and customers with your entire organisation. Customer buying habits, particular needs, interests and other data can be stored in a central location and easily shared.

5. Share the commitment. Nothing can prove more destructive to a commitment to extraordinary service than management for whom the concept is little more than lip service. Walk the walk by buying into that commitment just as much as you hope your people will. Make sure you reward top performance. Invest the time and expense in any sort of training that may help employees carry out and maintain high performance standards. Don't forget yourself and others in the front office. "Make sure that training takes in everyone, not just sales, marketing and other front line employees," says Karen Leland, author of "*Customer Service for Dummies*." "Training is an important part of creating a lifelong culture for service excellence since it helps build an understanding of the concept of service. And that means a top-down commitment. Leadership should set the tone for the entire effort."
6. Don't expect magic overnight. Another potential hurdle to extraordinary service is the expectation that it's like flicking a light switch — on it goes, and everything's hunky dory. Truth is, exceptional service takes time to take hold in an organisation, particularly one with an array of people and departments. Give it enough time. Review performance every four to six months. "It's essential to stay the course so you can improve service ratings," says Elaine Berke, a consultant.
7. Expect snafus and react accordingly. The road to top notch service is not without its bumps. Don't pretend they're not there. Rather, make them a part of the journey by acknowledging a slip up and, in so doing, recommitting to extraordinary performance.

BIBLIOGRAPHY

Albrecht, K., *Service Within. Solving the Middle Management Leadership Crisis*, Business One Irwin, Homewood, IL., 1990.

Blodgett, Jeffrey G., David L. Wakefield, and James H. Barnes., "The Effects of Customer Service on Consumer Complaining Behavior," *Journal of Services Marketing* 9: 31-42, 1995.

Booher, Dianna Daniels, *Communicate with confidence!: how to say it right the first time and every time*, New York: McGraw-Hill, 1994.

Bounds, Andy,*The jelly effect: how to make your communication stick*, Chichester, UK: Capstone, 2007.

Bradley Gale, Robert Chapman Wood, *Managing Customer Value: Creating Quality & Service That Customers Can See*, 1994.

Buchanan, R. and Gilles, C., "Value managed relationship: The key to customer retention and profitability", *European Management Journal*, vol. 8, no 4, 1990.

Buckinx W., Geert Verstraeten, and Dirk Van den Poel , "Predicting customer loyalty using the internal transactional database," *Expert Systems with Applications*, 32 (1), 2007.

Carrol, P. and Reichheld, F., "The fallacy of customer retention", *Journal of Retail Banking*, vol 13. no. 4, 1992.

Conway, Kelly, *Building Customer Relationships in the Electronic Age*, Chicago, IL: Technology Solutions Company.

Cusack, Michael, *Online Customer Care: Applying Today's Technology to Achieve World-Class Customer Interaction*, Milwaukee, WI: ASQ Quality Press.

Davis, T.R.V., "Satisfying internal customers", *Planning Review*, Vol. 20 No.1, 1992, pp. 34-7.

Dawkins, P. and Reichheld, F., "Customer retention as a competitive weapon", *Directors and Boards*, vol. 14, no. 4, 1990.

Ellis, Richard, *Communication skills: stepladders to success for the professional*, Bristol: Intellect Books, 2002.

Evenson, R., *Customer Service Training 101: Quick and easy techniques*, 2005.

Faruqui, Ahmad and Stephen George, "Quantifying Customer Response to Dynamic Pricing", *The Electricity Journal*, 2005.

Fornell, C. and Wernerfet, B., "Defensive marketing strategy by customer complaint management : a theoretical analysis", *Journal of Marketing*, 1987.

Genua, Robert L., *Managing your mouth: an owner's manual for your most important business asset*, New York: AMACOM Books, 1992.

Goldman, C., N. Hopper, R. Bharvirkar, B. Neenan, R. Boisvert, P. Cappers, D.Pratt, and K. Butkins, "Customer Strategies for Responding to Day-AheadMarket Hourly Electricity Pricing", August, 2005.

Goodman, G. S., *Monitoring, measuring and managing customer service*, San Francisco: Jossey-Bass, 2000.

Gordon, Ian, *Relationship Marketing: New Strategies, Techniques and Technologies to Win the Customers You Want and Keep Them Forever*, Toronto, ON: John Wiley and Sons.

Guirdham, Maureen,*Communication across cultures at work*, West Lafayette: Ichor Books, 2005.

Harari, O., "Should internal customers exist?", *Management Review*, Vol. 80 No. 7, 1991, pp. 41-3.

______________ , "Internal customer RIP", *Management Review*, Vol. 82 No. 6, 1993, pp. 30-1.

Hermon, P., Nitecki, D., Danuta, A., & Altman, E., "Service quality and customer satisfaction: An assessment and future directions", *Journal of Academic Librarianship*, 1999.

Klose, Allen, and Todd Finkle., "Service Quality and the Congruency of Employee Perceptions and Customer Expectations: The Case of an Electric Utility," *Psychology and Marketing* 12: 637-46, October 1995.

Moloney, Chris X., "Winning Your Customer's Loyalty: The Best Tools, Techniques and Practices" AMA Workshop Event(s), Misc. materials distributed related to event(s), San Diego, 2006.

Moore, Bloomfield H., *Sensible etiquette of the best society: customs, manners, morals, and home culture,* Philadelphia: Porter & Coates, 1878.

Morris, Charles, *The standard book of etiquette: what to do, what to say, what to write, what to wear,* United States: W.E. Scull, 1901.

Morton, Agnes H., *Etiquette: good manners for all people,* Philadelphia: Penn Pub. Co., 1919.

National Performance Review., "Serving the American Public: Best Practices in Resolving Customer Complaints", *Federal Benchmarking Consortium Study Report*, Washington, DC: U.S. Government Printing Office, 1996.

Parker, Ida White, *Office etiquette for business women,* New York: The Ronald Press Company, 1924

Post, Emily, *Etiquette in society, in business, in politics and at home.* New York and London: Funk & Wagnalls company, 1922.

Reichheld, F., *The Loyalty Effect,* Harvard Business School Press, Boston, 1996.

Reichheld, F. and Sasser, W., "Zero defects: quality comes to services", *Harvard Business Review*, Sept-Oct, 1990, pp 105-111.

Reid, Lillian N. *Personality and etiquette,* Boston: Little, 1941.

Richardson, Anna Steese Sausser, *Standard etiquette,* New York London: Harper & Brothers., 1925.

Rives, Hallie Erminie, *The modern and complete book of etiquette,* Philadelphia etc: The John C. Winston Co., 1939.

Schlesinger, L. and Heskett, J., "Breaking the cycle of failure in service", *Sloan Management Review*, spring, 1991, pp. 17-28.

Sheldon, L. W., *Sheldon's Twentieth century guide to etiquette: an accurate and up-to-date guide to modern etiquette,* Philadelphia: D. McKay, 1901.

Spector, Robert, and Patrick D. McCarthy., "The Nordstrom Way: The Inside Story of America's #1 Customer Service Company", New York: Wiley, 1995.

Stalcup, Gean., "Teamwork: A Real Story in Customer Needs at ITW Paslode," *Industrial Engineering* 25: 59, November 1993.

Stern, Renée Bernd, *Standard book of etiquette: social forms and good manners for all occasions,* Chicago: Laird, 1924.

Stevens, Carilyn, *Etiquette in daily living,* Chicago: Associated authors service, 1934.

Stieb, James A., "Clearing Up the Egoist Difficulty with Loyalty", *Journal of Business Ethics,* vol 63, no 1, 2006.

Stone, Douglas, *Difficult conversations: how to discuss what matters most*, New York: Penguin Books, 1999.

Zemke, R., Zemke, S., "Partnering: a new slant on serving the internal customer", *Training*, Vol. 31 No.10, 1994, pp. 37-43.

Zemke, Ron, "Winning Strategies: The 10 Commandments of Customer Service," *Incentive* 169: 81-83, November 1995.

_____________ and John A., Woods, eds., *Best Practices in Customer Service*, New York, AMACOM, 1999.

INDEX

Other Books on
MANAGEMENT SERIES

1. Be a Better Project Manager **(New)**
2. Be a Better Problem Solver **(New)**
3. Be a Better Motivator **(New)**
4. Be a Better Time Manager **(New)**
5. Effective Director
6. Network Marketing
7. Art of Entrepreneurship
8. How to Beat Your Competitors
9. How to Negotiate Effectively
10. Make Your Boss Happy
11. Art of Advertising
12. Art of Marketing
13. Art of Growing Business
14. Art of Retailing
15. Art of Leadership
16. Art of Team Building
17. Art of Corporate Communication
18. Art of Organisational Management
19. Improve your Marketing and Grow your Business
20. What Customers Really Want
21. Effective Presentation
22. The Right Decision Every Time

Lotus
PRESS